PLUMBING 101

25 Repairs & Projects You _Really_ Can Do

DAVID GRIFFIN

Creative Publishing international

CHANHASSEN, MINNESOTA
www.creativepub.com

Creative Publishing
international

Copyright © 2006
Creative Publishing international, Inc.
18705 Lake Drive East
Chanhassen, Minnesota 55317
1-800-328-3895
www.creativepub.com

Printed in Singapore

10 9 8 7 6 5 4 3 2 1

President/CEO: Ken Fund

Publisher: Bryan Trandem

Author: David Griffin
Editor: Mark Johanson
Art Director: David Schelitzche
Cover Design: Howard Grossman
Book Design: Richard Oriolo
Page Layout: Kari Johnston
Assistant Managing Editor: Tracy Stanley
Photo Acquisitions Editor: Julie Caruso
Production Manager: Laura Hokkanen

Library of Congress Cataloging-in-Publication Data

Griffin, David
Plumbing 101 : 25 repairs & projects you really
can do / by David Griffin.
 p. cm.
 Summary: "Includes 25 of the most common
plumbing projects and repairs and gives readers
everything they need to know to finish each
project safely, quickly, and with perfect results"--
Provided by publisher.
 ISBN-13: 978-1-58923-278-5 (soft cover)
 ISBN-10: 1-58923-278-X (soft cover)
 1. Plumbing--Amateurs' manuals. I. Title:
Plumbing one hundred one. II. Title.
 TH6124.G75 2006
 696'.1--dc22
                                    2006000669

NOTICE TO READERS

For safety, use caution, care and good judgment when following the procedures described in this book. The Publisher and
Black & Decker cannot assume responsibility for any damage
to property or injury to persons as a result of misuse of the
information provided.

The techniques shown in this book are general techniques for
various applications. In some instances, additional techniques
not shown in this book may be required. Always follow manufacturers' instructions included with products, since deviating
from the directions may void warranties. The projects in this
book vary widely as to skill levels required: some may not be
appropriate for all do-it-yourselfers, and some may require professional help.

Consult your local Building Department for information on
building permits, codes and other laws as they apply to your
project.

CONTENTS

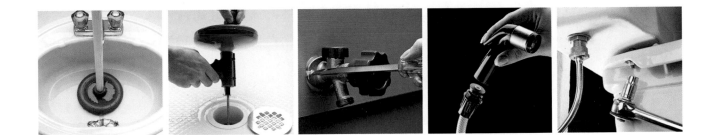

Welcome to Plumbing
101

LET'S FACE IT, PLUMBERS SPEND A LOT OF TIME FISHING SOCKS OUT OF TOILETS AND REPLACING 5-CENT WASHERS ON DRIPPY FAUCETS. NOTHING WRONG WITH THAT, EXCEPT THEY CHARGE $100 AN HOUR AND PROMISE TO MEET YOU AT THE DOOR "OH, SOMETIME BETWEEN 10 AND 3 O'CLOCK." WE THINK YOU HAVE BETTER WAYS TO SPEND YOUR TIME AND MONEY.

Look at the Table of Contents of *Plumbing 101*, and you'll find salt-of-the earth repairs and replacements—the kind of projects you need to keep your house running smoothly and looking good. Most important, they're doable.

Plumbing 101 is part of a new series of Black & Decker books that starts at square one. Unlike legions of other books on the trades, we present step-by-step repair and replacement instructions that assume no prior how-to knowledge. In *Plumbing 101*, we won't expect you to know where your water turns off or even what a water pipe looks like. We'll tell you. Period. If it's old news, skip ahead.

The 25 repair and replacement projects covered in this book involve a few basic tools and the ability to follow directions. If you skipped Vocational Ed. in high school, no problem, you're forgiven. We're replacing a toilet, not plumbing the *Queen Mary*.

The trick with any successful do-it-yourself project lies in identifying those jobs that you can complete without resorting to professional help (mechanical or psychiatric). Again, the 101 Series to the rescue. We've pre-screened projects to minimize chance of failure, property damage, and injury.

The *Plumbing 101* book will not ask you to use a torch. You will not need to smear molten metals on pipes hot enough to brand cattle. You will not be encouraged to re-plumb your bathroom, build a granite island sink in your kitchen, or install a multi-zone irrigation system in your backyard.

Hey, those are all wonderful projects, but they don't fit into the mission of this book. Here, we aim to provide practical information for practical people who don't have the time or inclination to take up plumbing as a second career.

On the following pages, we'll walk you through projects you can do. We'll let you know when a job might get hairy. And we'll show you, in photographs, what each step in a project looks like.

HERE'S HOW TO USE THIS BOOK:

The first two pages of most projects give necessary background information. You'll examine how things fit together and work, learn techniques, get an idea of how long the project might take, and see all the tools and materials you'll need to do a project.

Then, turn the page and begin. Virtually every step is photographed so you'll see exactly how to do the work, and along the way you'll find helpful sidebars that show you what to do if something unexpected happens, tips for using tools correctly, safety recommendations, and more. Before you know it, you'll notch up another home repair success.

The Home Plumbing System

A TYPICAL HOME PLUMBING SYSTEM INCLUDES THREE BASIC PARTS: a water supply system, a fixture and appliance set, and a drain system. These three parts can be seen clearly in the photograph of the cut-away house on the opposite page.

Fresh water enters a home through a main supply line (1). This fresh water source is provided by either a municipal water company or a private underground well. If the source is a municipal supplier, the water passes through a meter (2) that registers the amount of water used. A family of four uses about 400 gallons of water each day.

Immediately after the main supply enters the house, a branch line splits off (3) and is joined to a water heater (4). From the water heater, a hot water line runs parallel to the cold water line to bring the water supply to fixtures and appliances throughout the house. Fixtures include sinks, bathtubs, showers, and laundry tubs. Appliances include water heaters, dishwashers, clothes washers, and water softeners. Toilets and exterior sillcocks are examples of fixtures that require only a cold water line.

The water supply to fixtures and appliances is controlled with faucets and valves. Faucets and valves have moving parts and seals that eventually may wear out or break, but they are easily repaired or replaced.

Waste water then enters the drain system. It first must flow past a trap (5), a U-shaped piece of pipe that holds standing water and prevents sewer gases from entering the home. Every fixture must have a drain trap.

The drain system works entirely by gravity, allowing waste water to flow downhill through a series of large-diameter pipes. These drain pipes are attached to a system of vent pipes. Vent pipes (6) bring fresh air to the drain system, preventing suction that would slow or stop drain water from flowing freely. Vent pipes usually exit the house at a roof vent (7).

All waste water eventually reaches a main waste and vent stack (8). The main stack curves to become a sewer line (9) that exits the house near the foundation. In a municipal system, this sewer line joins a main sewer line located near the street. Where sewer service is not available, waste water empties into a septic system.

Water meter and main shutoff valves are located where the main water supply pipe enters the house. The water meter is the property of your local municipal water company. If the water meter leaks, or if you suspect it is not functioning properly, call your water company for repairs.

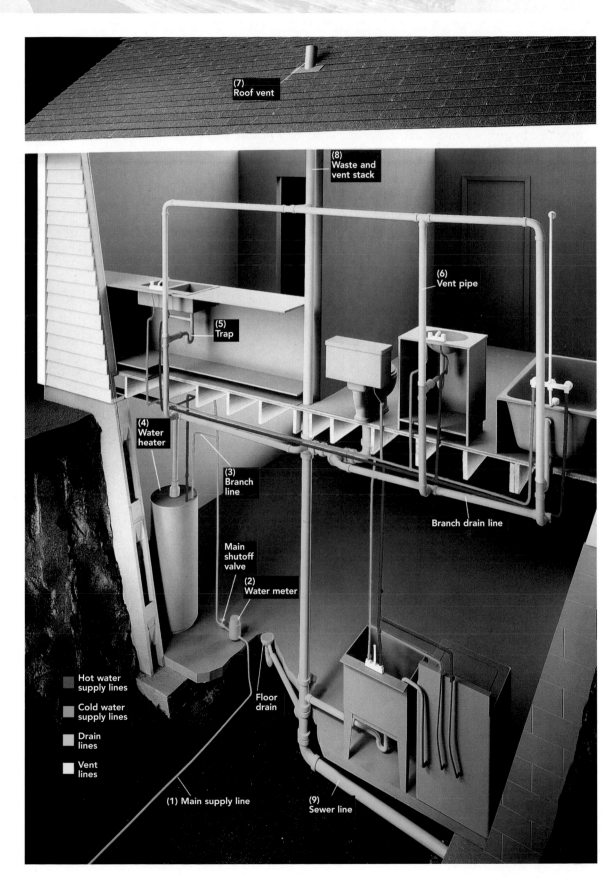

(7) Roof vent

(8) Waste and vent stack

(6) Vent pipe

(5) Trap

(4) Water heater

(3) Branch line

Main shutoff valve

(2) Water meter

Branch drain line

Hot water supply lines

Cold water supply lines

Drain lines

Vent lines

Floor drain

(1) Main supply line

(9) Sewer line

WATER SUPPLY SYSTEM

Water supply pipes carry hot and cold water throughout a house. In homes built before 1960, the original supply pipes are usually made of galvanized iron. Newer homes have supply pipes made of copper. In most areas of the country, supply pipes made of rigid plastic or PEX are accepted by local plumbing codes. Water supply pipes are made to withstand the high pressures of the water supply system. They have small diameters, usually ½" to ¾", and are joined with strong, watertight fittings. The hot and cold lines run in tandem to all parts of the house. Usually, the supply pipes run inside wall cavities or are strapped to the undersides of floor joists.

Hot and cold water supply pipes are connected to fixtures or appliances. Fixtures include sinks, tubs, and showers. Some fixtures, such as toilets or hose bibs, are supplied only by cold water. Appliances include dishwashers and clothes washers. Tradition says that hot water supply pipes and faucet handles are found on the left-hand side of a fixture, with cold water on the right.

Because it is pressurized, the water supply system is prone to leaks. This is especially true of galvanized iron pipe, which has limited resistance to corrosion.

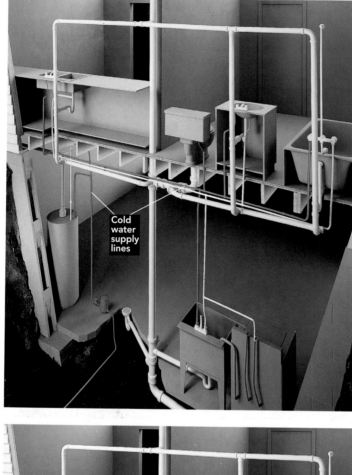

Cold water supply lines

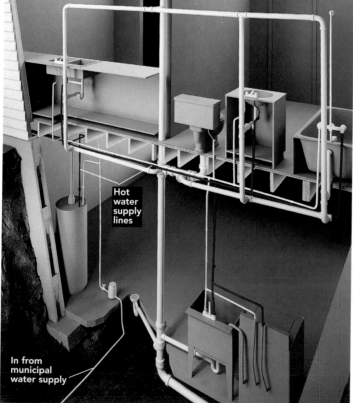

Hot water supply lines

In from municipal water supply

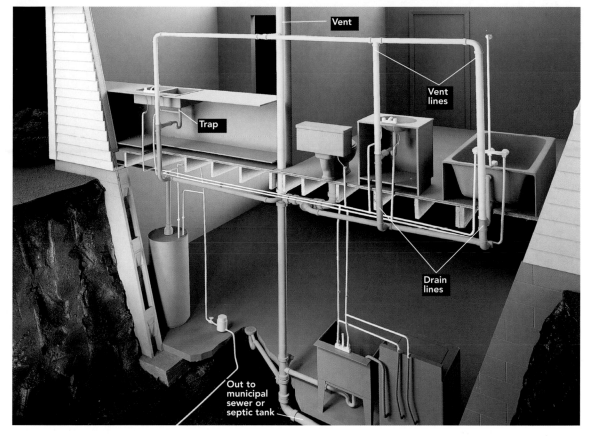

DRAIN-WASTE-VENT SYSTEM

Drain pipes use gravity to carry waste water away from fixtures, appliances, and other drains. This waste water is carried out of the house to a municipal sewer system or septic tank.

Drain pipes are usually plastic or cast iron. In some older homes, drain pipes may be made of copper or lead. Because they are not part of the supply system, lead drain pipes pose no health hazard. However, lead pipes are no longer manufactured for home plumbing systems.

Drain pipes have diameters ranging from 1½" to 4". These large diameters allow waste water to pass through easily.

Traps are an important part of the drain system. These curved sections of drain pipe hold standing water, and they are usually found near any drain opening. The standing water of a trap prevents sewer gases from backing up into the home. Each time a drain is used, the standing trap water is flushed away and is replaced by new water.

In order to work properly, the drain system requires air. Air allows waste water to flow freely down drain pipes.

To allow air into the drain system, drain pipes are connected to vent pipes. All drain systems must include vents, and the entire system is called the drain-waste-vent (DWV) system. One or more vent stacks, located on the roof, provide the air needed for the DWV system to work.

Plumbing Tools

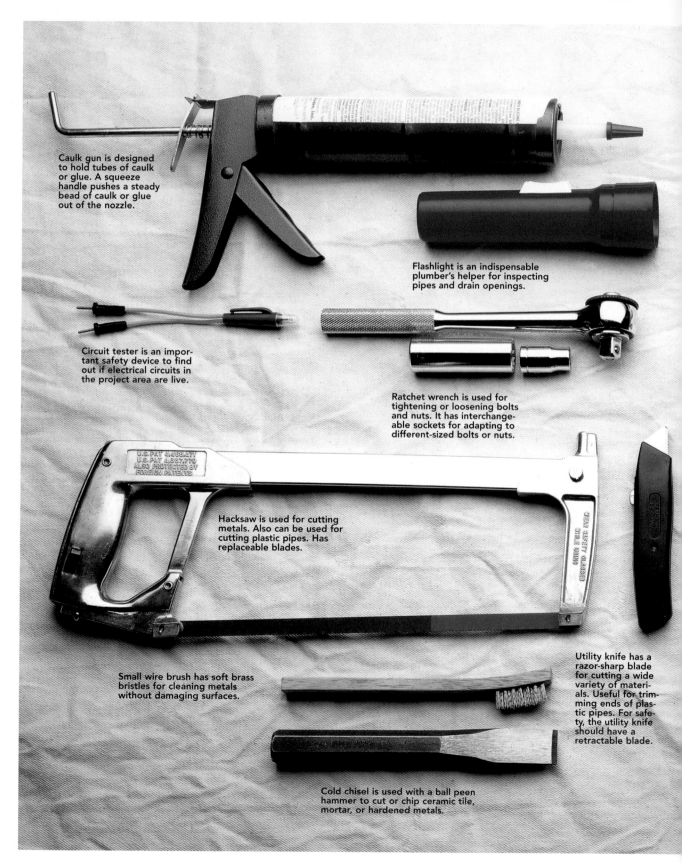

Caulk gun is designed to hold tubes of caulk or glue. A squeeze handle pushes a steady bead of caulk or glue out of the nozzle.

Flashlight is an indispensable plumber's helper for inspecting pipes and drain openings.

Circuit tester is an important safety device to find out if electrical circuits in the project area are live.

Ratchet wrench is used for tightening or loosening bolts and nuts. It has interchangeable sockets for adapting to different-sized bolts or nuts.

Hacksaw is used for cutting metals. Also can be used for cutting plastic pipes. Has replaceable blades.

Small wire brush has soft brass bristles for cleaning metals without damaging surfaces.

Utility knife has a razor-sharp blade for cutting a wide variety of materials. Useful for trimming ends of plastic pipes. For safety, the utility knife should have a retractable blade.

Cold chisel is used with a ball peen hammer to cut or chip ceramic tile, mortar, or hardened metals.

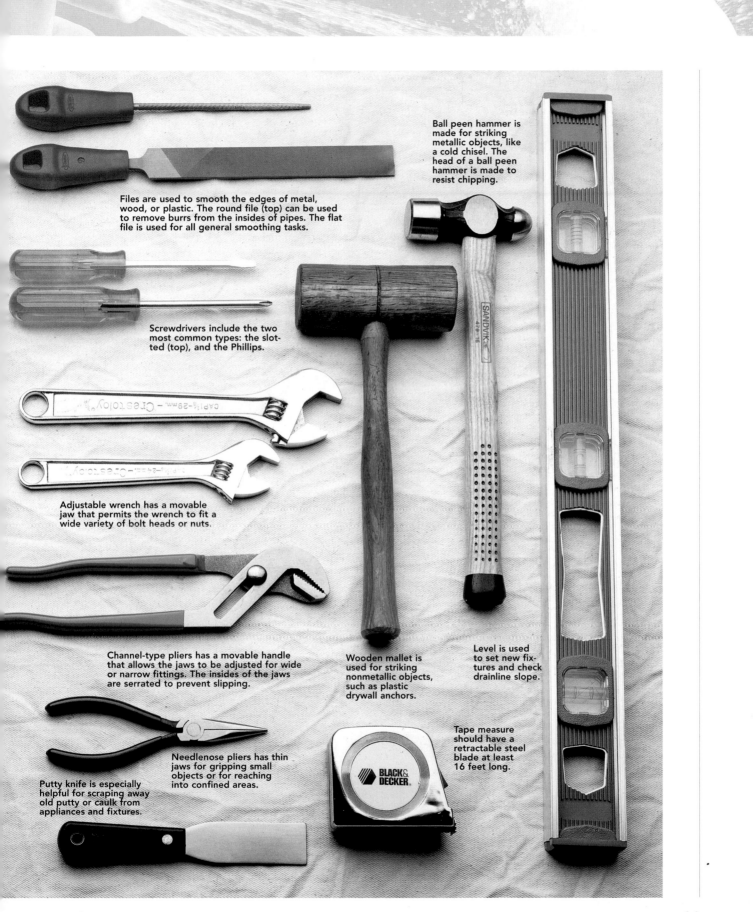

Ball peen hammer is made for striking metallic objects, like a cold chisel. The head of a ball peen hammer is made to resist chipping.

Files are used to smooth the edges of metal, wood, or plastic. The round file (top) can be used to remove burrs from the insides of pipes. The flat file is used for all general smoothing tasks.

Screwdrivers include the two most common types: the slotted (top), and the Phillips.

Adjustable wrench has a movable jaw that permits the wrench to fit a wide variety of bolt heads or nuts.

Channel-type pliers has a movable handle that allows the jaws to be adjusted for wide or narrow fittings. The insides of the jaws are serrated to prevent slipping.

Wooden mallet is used for striking nonmetallic objects, such as plastic drywall anchors.

Level is used to set new fixtures and check drainline slope.

Needlenose pliers has thin jaws for gripping small objects or for reaching into confined areas.

Tape measure should have a retractable steel blade at least 16 feet long.

Putty knife is especially helpful for scraping away old putty or caulk from appliances and fixtures.

Pipe wrenches have a movable jaw that adjusts to fit a variety of pipe diameters. They can be rented.

Closet auger is used to clear toilet clogs. A bend in the tube allows the auger to be positioned in the bottom of the toilet bowl. The bend is usually protected with a rubber sleeve to prevent scratching the toilet.

Spud wrench is specially designed for removing or tightening large nuts, mostly on toilets.

Plunger clears drain clogs with water and air pressure. A flanged plunger used to clear toilet traps is shown here (the flap is folded up for clearing sink and shower lines).

Hand auger, sometimes called a snake, is used to clear clogs in drain lines. A long, flexible steel cable is stored in the disk-shaped crank. A pistol-grip handle allows the user to apply steady pressure on the cable.

Useful power tools include a cordless screwdriver, reciprocating saw, and drill/driver.

PLUMBING MATERIALS

Check local plumbing code
for materials allowed in
your area. Common pipe
types include:

A) Cast iron for main
drain stack

B) ABS drain pipe
(no longer allowed)

C) PVC drain pipe

D) Chromed brass
fixture drain pipe

E) CPVC supply pipe

F) Galvanized supply
pipe (seldom used)

G) Rigid copper
supply tube

H) Chromed copper
fixture supply pipe

I) PE plastic supply tube
(mostly used in irrigation)

J) Flexible copper
supply tube

K) PEX (cross-linked
polyethylene) flexible
supply line

A

B

C

D

E

F

G

H

K

I

J

Evaluating Your Plumbing

You don't have to possess the knowledge and experience of a journeyman plumber to do some basic evaluations of your plumbing system. Taking a few moments to examine the system helps you learn which parts are which and identify any parts of your system that may be in disrepair or hold the potential for future problems.

The tips on the next page offer a bit of guidance on how to be a home plumbing sleuth. By following them you can quickly and accurately identify cold and hot supply lines, drain lines, the water main, and shutoff valve locations. And the tips below will help you test your water supply capacity to find out if the pressure and volume are adequate to meet your water needs.

Fixture Units	Minimum Gallons per Minute (GPM)
10	8
15	11
20	14
25	17
30	20

Minimum recommended water capacity is based on total demand on the system, as measured by fixture units, a standard of measurement assigned by the plumbing code. First, add up the total units of all the fixtures in your plumbing system (see chart above). Then, perform the water supply capacity test described below. Finally, compare your water capacity with the recommended minimums listed above. If it falls below that recommended GPM, then the main water supply pipe running from the city water main to your home is inadequate and should be replaced with a larger pipe by a licensed contractor.

HOW TO DETERMINE YOUR WATER SUPPLY CAPACITY

1 Shut off the water at the valve on your main water meter, run a faucet on every floor to empty the supply lines, and then disconnect the pipe on the house side of the meter. You can do this by counter-rotating the large nuts on the line with two pipe wrenches (you can rent these if you don't want to invest in a pair).

2 Make a downspout like the one seen above from 2" PVC pipe sections and position it over the water line to direct water down into a garbage can. Open the main supply valve and let the water run for 30 seconds. Shut off the water, then measure the water in the container by bailing with a 1-gallon container. Multiply this figure by two to find your water capacity in gallons per minute (GPM).

HOW TO INSPECT YOUR PLUMBING

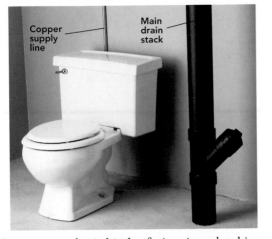

Copper supply line

Main drain stack

There are two basic kinds of pipes in a plumbing system: supply pipes and drain pipes. Supply pipes are always full of water under pressure and drain pipes (which include vent pipes that only move air) are empty when not in use. Supply pipes usually are ½" or ¾" in diameter and drain pipes are anywhere from 1½" to 4" or more. The largest drain pipes are the main drain stack (multi-level houses) and horizontal house drains fed by branch lines.

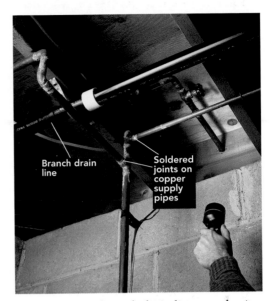

Branch drain line

Soldered joints on copper supply pipes

In your basement, branch drain lines run horizontally at a very low slope and ultimately feed into the main drain stack or house drain. They enter the basement through the floor, usually directly under walls. Look for moisture or discoloration around joints. On copper supply lines, visually inspect the soldered joints for pinholes or other signs of deterioration.

Trace hot water pipes from the water heater (the outlet side will be labeled "Hot" on the appliance). Hot supply lines will be hot to the touch when the fixture they connect to is in use.

Heat duct

To identify which supply pipes feed which fixture, you can sometimes measure from the fixture to a heating register. Then, locate the ductwork directly below the register and measure out from it and look for supply lines.

Shutting Off the Water

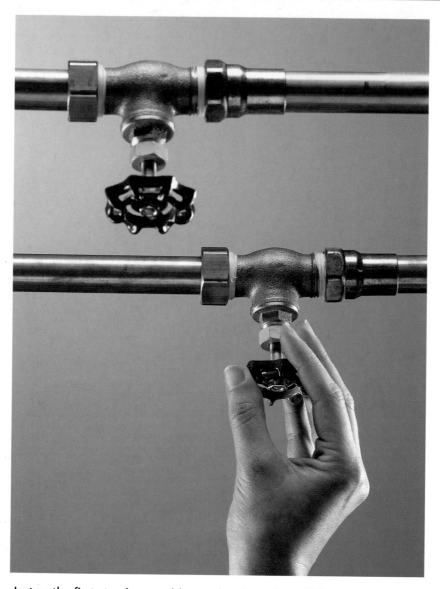

1

Just as the first step in any wiring project is to shut off the power at the main service panel, most plumbing projects begin with shutting off the water supply at one of the shutoff valves in the plumbing system.

USUALLY THERE ARE TWO OR THREE WAYS TO TURN OFF THE WATER. First, try to close the stop valves at the fixture or appliance that's broken. If these are damaged or absent, turn off the water at intermediate shutoff valves that control the hot and cold water to the part of the house with the problem. The whole hot water system usually can be turned off near the hot water heater. Finally, you can stop the water to the entire house at a main shutoff located near the water meter. As a last resort, your municipal water works can shut off your water before it gets to your house. If you have a well, find the shutoff on the pipe between the pressure tank and the rest of your plumbing.

WATER STOP VALVES 101

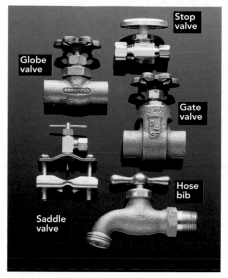

Access panel with door opens to shut-offs for tub/shower

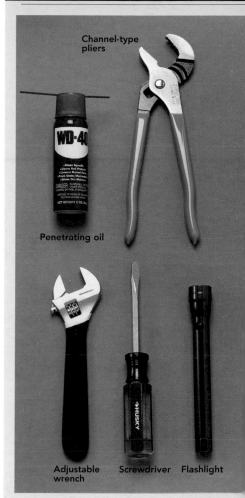

Channel-type pliers

WD-40

Penetrating oil

Adjustable wrench   Screwdriver   Flashlight

Water stop valves and shutoff valves function much like faucets, except most of them are left open all the time. Unfortunately, valves used on potable water (water for drinking and cooking) lines may be similar to valves used on natural gas lines, heating oil pipes, and hot water heating pipes. Finding the valves you need may require some careful tracing of pipes from a fixture back to the water meter. The photos here show common water shutoff valves.

SKILLS YOU'LL NEED

- Using locking pliers
- Loosening stuck valve handles

TERMS YOU NEED TO KNOW

VALVE—any device that regulates the flow of fluids or gases through a pipe.

STOP VALVE—a valve used to stop hot or cold water to a single faucet, toilet, or appliance.

INTERMEDIATE SHUTOFF VALVE—a valve on a pipe used to stop hot or cold water to part of a house or building; often a gate valve or globe valve.

HOT WATER SHUTOFF VALVE—a valve that shuts off cold water supply to the hot water tank.

MAIN SHUTOFF VALVE—a valve that shuts off all the water to a house or building.

DIFFICULTY LEVEL

SKILLS LEVEL

EASY   MODERATE

Time: A few minutes to ½ hour

HOW TO SHUT OFF HOT AND COLD WATER

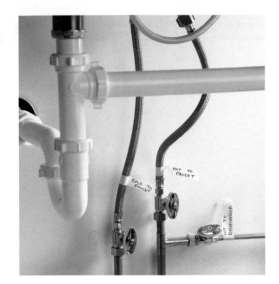

1 Try to shut off the water locally first. Toilets and sinks usually have stop valves under them. Tubs and showers may have hot and cold shutoffs on the faucet itself or through a wall access panel in a room adjoining the bathroom. Washing machines are connected to shutoff valves with hot and cold supply hoses. Dishwashers sometimes share a two-outlet shutoff with the hot water supply tube for the kitchen faucet.

2 If you can't locate or operate the stop valve, look for intermediate shutoffs that control multiple fixtures in a supply line. Finding the right intermediate shutoff(s) can require trial and error and detective work. Hot water pipes will always lead back to a hot water heater and cold water pipes will lead back to a water meter (below) or a well pressure tank.

3 The hot water shutoff is located at or near the water heater and lets you turn off all the hot water in the house. There will usually be a valve on the pipe supplying cold water to the heater, and there may also be a valve on the outgoing pipe from the heater. If your water is heated by gas, do not be confused by the gas pipe and gas shutoff. The gas pipe leads to the thermostat at the bottom of the water heater.

4 The main water shutoff will be located near the water meter, generally found in your basement. Do not confuse it with the gas meter shutoff, which has a disc shaped device associated with it and generally turns off with a wrench or lever, rather than by hand-spinning. In an emergency, your municipal water works may be contacted to shut off the water with a key (a special wrench) between the public water main on the street and your house. NOTE: Some municipal water works do not meter water use.

What if the valve is stuck?

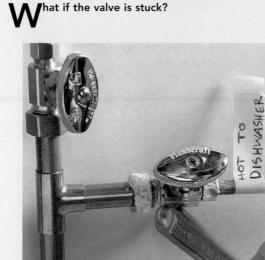

1 Stop valves and shutoff valves may become fused by corrosion if they are not used regularly. If your valve won't operate, rap lightly on the valve body with a wrench handle or hammer and try again to turn the handle clockwise.

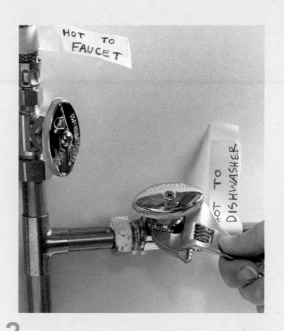

2 If rapping the valve doesn't work, try loosening the packing nut with your adjustable wrench until it leaks just a little bit of water. Then, retighten the nut and try the handle again.

3 If the valve handle won't turn the stem, remove it so you can grip the valve stem directly. Start by unscrewing the screw that secures the handle to the valve. Remove the screw and the handle.

4 Grip the end of the handle stem with channel-type pliers or locking pliers and twist clockwise. Don't overdo it; you can break the valve and create a flood.

2

Lost Down the Drain?
Opening the Trap

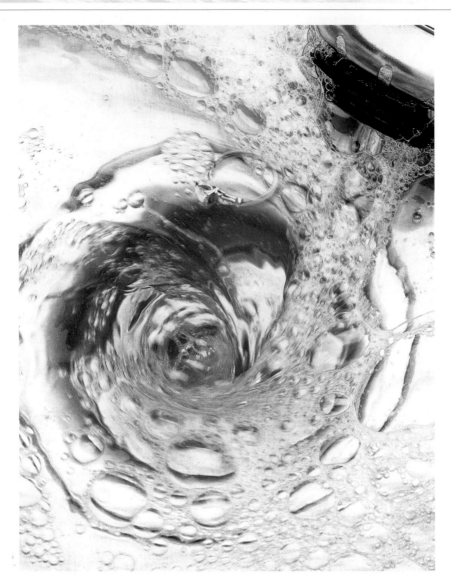

Your wedding ring fell down the drain? Don't panic yet. Chances are good that the P-trap caught it.

EVERY PLUMBING FIXTURE IN YOUR HOUSE HAS A TRAP—a downward facing drainage loop that can collect small, heavy items (like wedding rings) that accidentally fall into the drain. The main function of a trap is not to catch rings, but to hold water. The water in a trap acts as a plug to keep sewer gases from rising into the house. Sink traps are located beneath the sink basin. Bathtub and shower traps are located near the drain and are sometimes accessible through a panel in an adjoining room. A toilet trap is an integral part of the fixture—the front part of the trap is the bowl itself. You can fish out an object from a toilet trap with coat-hanger wire since the bend only goes back a little way from the visible side before bending up again. But if an object is swept out of a trap, it has embarked on a journey through the sewer system, and you may be out of luck.

TRAPS 101

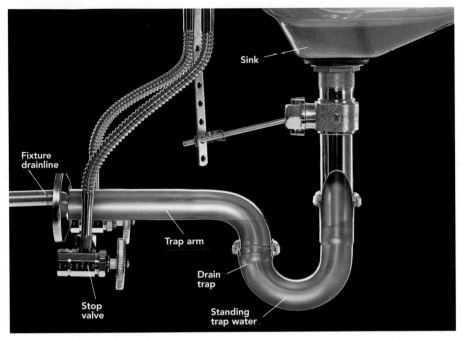

Sink
Fixture drainline
Stop valve
Trap arm
Drain trap
Standing trap water

A *drain trap* is a section of pipe attached near the top of a *fixture drain* that loops downward and then upward again. This creates a "trap" for water that blocks sewer gases from rising up though your drainlines and out the drain opening of a *fixture.* It also creates a blockage point for debris and a catch basin for small objects that find their way into the drain opening. Traps are designed to be easy to take apart for cleaning or retrieval.

TERMS YOU NEED TO KNOW

TRAP—downward bend in a drain in or near a fixture that can catch small objects. The standing water in a trap keeps sewer gases from rising into the house.

S-TRAP—The S-shaped trap is an older design used when the waste pipe comes out of the floor.

P-TRAP—Modern sink, tub, and shower traps are shaped like a P tipped on its face.

J-BEND—also called a "drain bend" or simply a "trap", this is the part that forms the low bend on a P-Trap or S-Trap.

TRAP ARM—also called a "wall tube," this extends from the J-bend to the trap adapter at the wall on a P-trap.

TRAP ADAPTER—also called a "drain pipe connector," this is a common transition fitting that lets you attach a light gauge chromed-brass or plastic trap arm to the larger heavy-gauge waste pipe coming out of the wall. It uses a washer and slip nut.

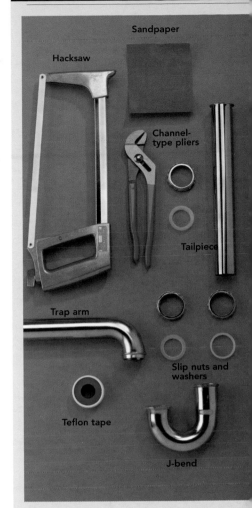

Hacksaw
Sandpaper
Channel-type pliers
Tailpiece
Trap arm
Slip nuts and washers
Teflon tape
J-bend

SKILLS YOU'LL NEED

• Unscrewing and retightening compression-style slip joints

DIFFICULTY LEVEL

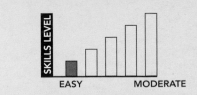

SKILLS LEVEL

EASY   MODERATE

Time: ½ hour to 1 hour

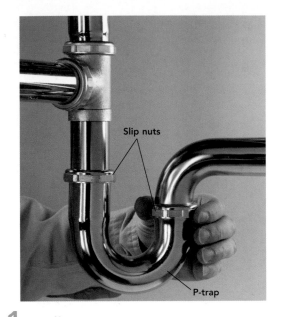

1 Before removing a sink trap, place a bucket under the trap to catch water that spills out. Loosen the slip nut at one end of the trap (a P-trap is seen here). Use channel-type pliers if the nut won't unscrew by hand.

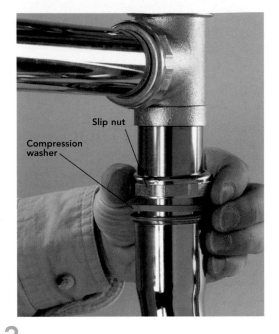

2 Loosen the slip nut on the other end of the trap and pull both nuts away from the union. You will find a compression washer at each union. Slide these back as well and remove the trap by pulling down on it.

3 Keep track of slip nuts and washers and note their up/down orientation. Clean out debris within the trap and examine it. If the trap or the slip nuts and washers are in poor repair (very common), purchase replacement parts, making sure they are made from the same material and are the same size as the rest of the trap.

4 Reassemble the trap pieces just as they came off, or follow instructions on replacement parts. If the trap is made of plastic, hand tighten only. Wrap Teflon tape onto the male threads of metal tubes and then tighten a quarter turn beyond hand tight with channel-type pliers. Tighten joints that leak.

What if your trap looks like this?

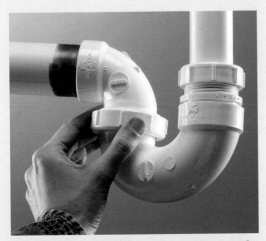

Some sink, tub, and shower traps are made out of the same heavy plastic (Schedule 40 PVC) or metal as the rest of your DWV plumbing and do not fit together like light plastic or chromed drain traps. But even if some parts are permanently fused together by a process called solvent-welding (these typically have a tell-tale purple band of color around the joint) you may still be able to access the trap by untwisting a union. Threaded joints are a sign that you've got a removable trap.

To access the trap, simply unscrew the joint fittings as on the previous page. Unlike a tubular trap, the nut at the DWV trap arm union unscrews counterclockwise from below. That's because the nut faces up instead of down. The slip nut on the fixture side of the trap is loosened like that of a tubular trap.

What if my trap is permanently solvent-welded to the drain and trap arm?

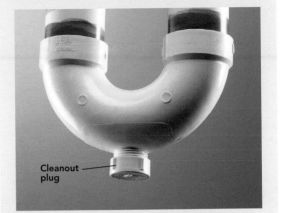

Cleanout plug

Often, bathtubs or showers have a drain trap system that is completely solvent-welded together, making it impossible to disassemble without cutting the pipes. But if you're lucky, the trap will have a cleanout plug at the bottom, like the one above.

The cleanout plug can be removed to clear the trap and retrieve lost items. Try hand-loosening the plug first, although unless your plumbing is virtually brand new you'll probably need an adjustable wrench to remove the plug. Fair warning—your hand is very likely to be drenched with fairly disgusting drain water, but hopefully, it will be worth it.

Maintaining Your Water Heater

3

A well-maintained water heater can last up to 20 years (if you're lucky as well as conscientious) and is also a much safer home appliance.

WATER HEATERS ARE THE SECOND BIGGEST CONSUMER OF ENERGY IN MOST HOMES (AFTER THE FURNACE). In fact, heating water is responsible for 4 percent of America's total energy consumption, according to the United States Geological Survey. It's easy to see that maintaining your water heater saves money, but it also protects your home and family. At their most basic, water heaters are containers filled with extremely hot water and fueled by gas burners or major amounts of electricity. It's worth taking the time to treat them with care.

WATER HEATERS 101

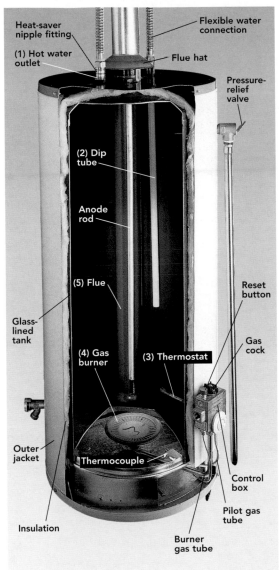

- Heat-saver nipple fitting
- Flexible water connection
- (1) Hot water outlet
- Flue hat
- Pressure-relief valve
- (2) Dip tube
- Anode rod
- (5) Flue
- Reset button
- Glass-lined tank
- (4) Gas burner
- (3) Thermostat
- Gas cock
- Thermocouple
- Outer jacket
- Control box
- Pilot gas tube
- Insulation
- Burner gas tube

How a gas water heater works: Hot water leaves the tank through the *hot water outlet* (1) as fresh, cold water enters the water heater through the *dip tube* (2). As the water temperature drops, the *thermostat* (3) opens the gas valve, and the *gas burner* (4) is lighted by a pilot flame. Exhaust gases are vented through the *flue* (5). When the water temperature reaches a preset temperature, the thermostat closes the gas valve, extinguishing the burner. The *thermocouple* protects against gas leaks by automatically shutting off the gas if the pilot flame goes out. An *anode rod* protects the tank lining from rust by attracting corrosive elements in the water. A *pressure-relief valve* guards against ruptures caused by steam buildup in the tank.

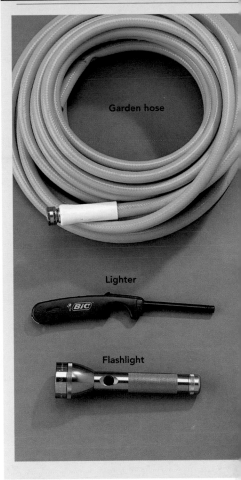

The best setting for a water heater is between 120° and 125°, or L for Low. If the thermostat's set too high, the water coming from your faucets can be hot enough to cause serious burns, especially on children or the elderly. To check the temperature, let the water run for a few minutes, then check it with a candy thermometer. Adjust the water heater's thermostat as necessary.

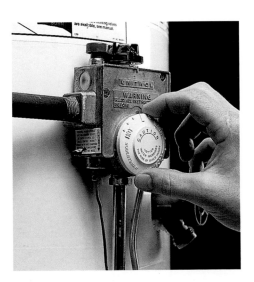

HOW TO FLUSH A WATER HEATER

1 First, turn off the heater. If you have a gas unit, set the gas valve on "Pilot." If it's electric, turn the circuit breaker to the Off position. Keep all children and pets away from the area.

2 Connect a garden hose to the drain valve at the bottom of the tank. Close the shutoff valve on the cold-water inlet. Open the temperature/pressure relief valve, and leave it open. Run the hose to a nearby sink or floor drain.

3 Open the drain valve at the bottom of the heater. Be careful: hot water will flow out. If the tank doesn't drain, sediment probably is clogging the drain valve. Close the pressure relief valve and turn on the cold water inlet valve. If it still doesn't drain, it's time to call a plumber. Keep an eye on the water coming out of the hose. When it runs clear, you've removed as much sediment as possible. Close the drain valve and disconnect the hose. Close the pressure relief valve and open up the cold-water inlet valve.

OPTION: If you have a water heater with a high enough tank drain valve, you may find it easier to simply drain the tank by opening the valve and letting the water run into a bucket.

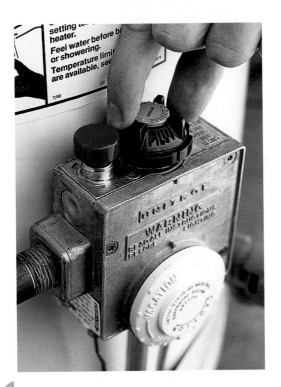

1 If the pilot light on your gas water heater goes out, here is how to re-light it. Turn the gas cock on top of the water heater control box to the "Pilot" position.

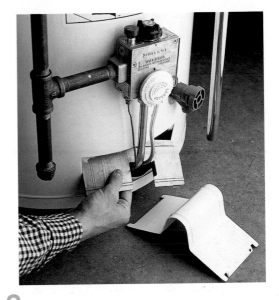

2 Remove the outer and inner access panels covering the burner chamber. With a flashlight, inspect inside the exposed chamber to make sure there are no cobwebs or other flammable debris. If you see anything that could catch fire, vacuum out the chamber with a shop vac.

3 Strike a flame (preferably a long fireplace match or lighter) and hold the flame next to the end of the pilot gas tube inside the burner chamber.

4 While holding the match next to the end of the gas tube, press the "Reset" button on top of the control box. When the pilot flame lights, continue to depress the "Reset" button for one minute. Then, turn the gas cock to the "On" position and replace the panels. If the pilot will not stay lit, your gas burner jets may need cleaning or the thermocouple might need to be replaced. Call a plumber or your public utility service and have a professional perform this job.

Fixing a Dripping Sink Faucet

4

Eventually, just about every faucet develops leaks and drips. Repairs can usually be accomplished simply by replacing the mechanical parts inside the faucet body (the main trick is figuring our which kind of parts your faucet has).

IT'S NOT SURPRISING THAT SINK FAUCETS LEAK AND DRIP. Any fitting that contains moving mechanical parts is susceptible to failure. But add to the equation the persistent force of water pressure working against the parts, and the real surprise is that faucets don't fail more quickly or often. It would be a bit unfair to say that the inner workings of a faucet are regarded as disposable by manufacturers, but it is safe to say that these parts have become more easy to remove and replace.

The most important aspect of sink faucet repair is identifying which type of faucet you own. In this chapter we show all of the common types and provide instructions on repairing them. In every case, the easiest and most reliable repair method is to purchase a replacement kit with brand new internal working parts for the model and brand of faucet you own.

SINK FAUCETS 101

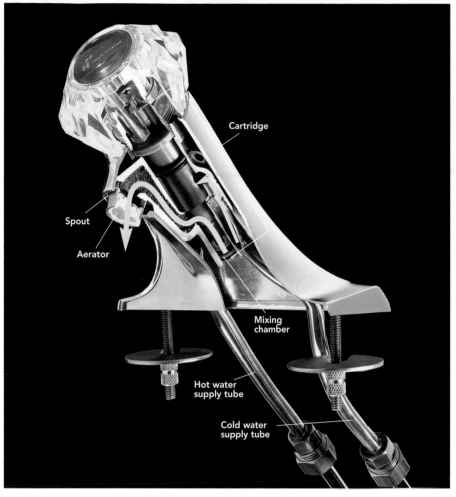

Cartridge

Spout

Aerator

Mixing chamber

Hot water supply tube

Cold water supply tube

Almost all leaks are caused by malfunctioning faucet valve mechanisms. Whether your sink faucet is a one-handle cartridge type (above) or a two-handle compression type or anything in between, the solution to fixing the leak is to clean or replace the parts that seal off the hot and cold water inlets from the spout.

TERMS YOU NEED TO KNOW

COMPRESSION VALVE—a valve type in which a spindle moves a washer up and down to stop or allow water flow through a valve seat.

CARTRIDGE VALVE—a valve type containing a cartridge, usually made of plastic or plastic and metal, in which a channel is slid open and closed by rotating a handle (see the example above).

NEOPRENE—a rubber-like, usually black material from which washers, rings, gaskets, and other seal-forming valve parts are made.

TELEPHONE—an invaluable tool used to contact your faucet's manufacturer, a font of information specific to the repair of your particular faucet.

TOOLS & SUPPLIES YOU'LL NEED

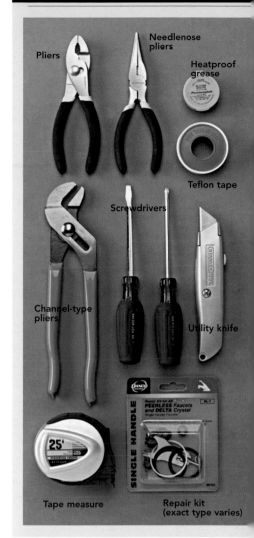

Pliers

Needlenose pliers

Heatproof grease

Teflon tape

Screwdrivers

Channel-type pliers

Utility knife

Tape measure

Repair kit (exact type varies)

SKILLS YOU'LL NEED

- Using channel-type pliers
- Tracking the order and arrangement of parts
- Phone or computer research

DIFFICULTY LEVEL

SKILLS LEVEL

EASY   MODERATE

Time: 30 minutes to 1 hour plus research and shopping

HOW TO FIX A COMPRESSION FAUCET

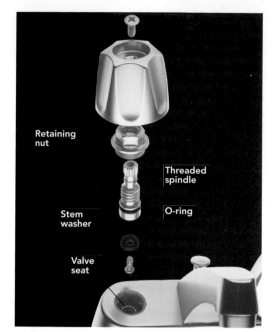

Retaining nut

Threaded spindle

O-ring

Stem washer

Valve seat

Most compression valves have a threaded metal spindle with a disc-shaped stem washer on the end. When the spindle is screwed all the way in, the stem washer covers a hole, and water flow to the spout is stopped. Drips from the spout happen when the seal between the stem washer and the rim of the hole (called the "valve seat") is imperfect. Usually, replacing the stem washer is enough to stop the drip.

Stem assembly

Faucet body

2 Use channel-type pliers to unscrew a retaining nut or the entire stem assembly from the faucet body. If what you find looks similar to the stem assembly shown in step 3, you're in the right place.

1 Turn off the water at the stop valves for the faucet you are fixing then open the faucet and let the water drain out. Remove the handles by prying an index cap off the top with a dull knife or screwdriver and removing the screw hidden underneath.

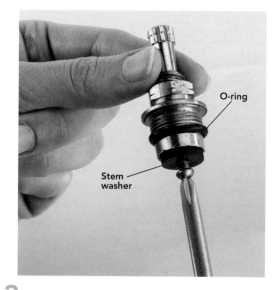

O-ring

Stem washer

3 Unscrew the stem screw and remove the stem washer. You must find an exact replacement. A flat washer should always be replaced with a flat washer, for example, even if a profiled washer fits. Your washer may have a size code printed on the back, but it's usually easiest to bring the whole stem into the hardware store or home center and try on new neoprene parts there.

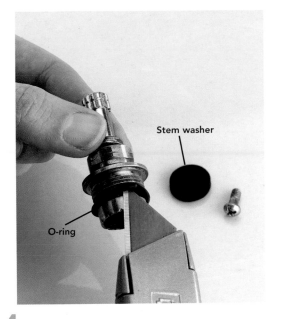

Stem washer

O-ring

4 Pry or cut off the O-ring on the stem with a utility knife. This keeps water from leaking under the handle when the faucet is on.

Aerator

6 Wrap Teflon tape onto the retaining nut threads and screw it onto the faucet body. Tighten lightly with channel-type pliers. Replace the handle, the handle screw, and the index cap. TIP: Unscrew the aerator at the tip of the spout and open the faucet before turning the water back on. This will flush debris from the system.

5 Coat the new O-ring and washer with heat-proof grease and install them. Tighten the stem screw enough to hold the washer in place, but do not distort the washer by overtightening. Coat the large threaded spindle threads with heatproof grease to lubricate the action of the faucet valve.

HERE'S HOW

There are many ways to classify sink faucets, but perhaps the most useful distinction is compression style versus washerless. These names refer to the type of mechanism inside the faucet. Many older faucets are compression type, but most newer ones are washerless, which can be one of three principal types: cartridge, ball, or disc. All one-handle faucets are washerless. The best way to tell if your faucet is a compression type or washerless is to turn the handle. With compression faucets you can feel the compression building as you crank the handle, even after the water flow has stopped. On washerless models, the handle comes to an abrupt stop.

HOW TO FIX A CARTRIDGE FAUCET

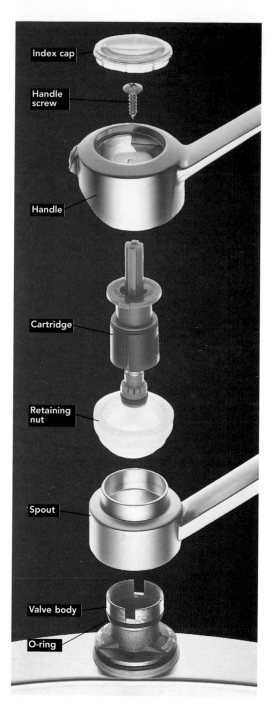

Index cap

Handle screw

Handle

Cartridge

Retaining nut

Spout

Valve body

O-ring

Index cap

1 Turn off the water at the stop valves. To avoid losing small parts, put a rag in the drain if it has no stopper. Some cartridge faucets have an index cap covering a handle screw. Other handles, especially on one-handle faucets, are secured with a recessed set screw that can be loosened with a $\frac{3}{32}$" or $\frac{7}{64}$" hex wrench. A lever type handle with no set screw may be removed with channel-type pliers.

SHOPPING TIP

Replacement cartridges are not interchangeable among brands or sometimes even among models from the same manufacturer. It's always a good idea to bring the old cartridge with you to the hardware store to help you select the correct replacement.

Both one- and two-handle faucets are available with replaceable plastic cartridges inside the faucet body. These cartridges (used by Price-Pfister, Sterling, Kohler, Moen, and others) regulate the flow of water through the spout, and in single-handle faucets they also mix the hot and cold water to alter the temperature out of the spout. To locate the correct replacement cartridge for your faucet, knowing the manufacturer and model number is a great help.

Retaining nut

2 Remove the retaining nut, if there is one, with channel-type pliers. A recessed nut with notches can be removed with open needlenose pliers or a tool provided by the faucet manufacturer. With other kinds, you'll remove a sleeve and three screws before extracting the cartridge.

3 Record the direction the cartridge is facing by noting the orientation of some distinctive part of the cartridge (some are cast with an orientation tab that generally should point straight forward). Pull the cartridge straight up and out with pliers. You may need to twist the cartridge back and forth to break the seal.

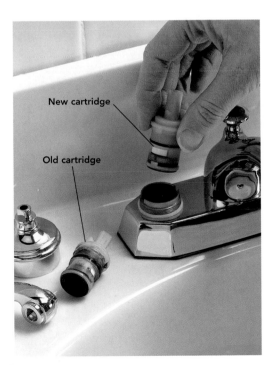

New cartridge

Old cartridge

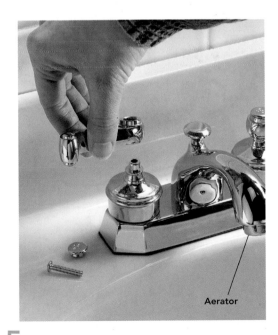

Aerator

4 Purchase a replacement cartridge. Apply heatproof grease to the valve seat and O-rings, then install the cartridge in the correct orientation and with its tabs seated in the slotted body of the faucet.

5 Reattach the handle, remove the aerator, turn on the water, and test. If the faucet doesn't work, the cartridge may be facing the wrong direction. Remove it and reinsert it facing the other way, still making sure the tabs fit into the slots on the valve body.

HOW TO FIX A BALL FAUCET

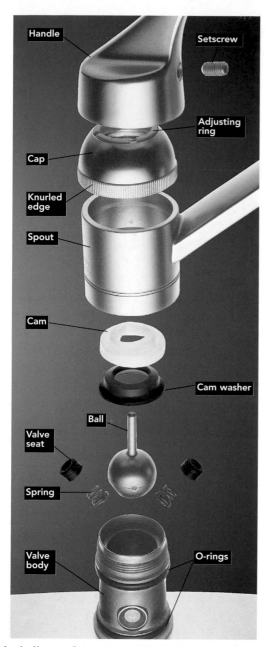

Handle
Setscrew
Adjusting ring
Cap
Knurled edge
Spout
Cam
Cam washer
Ball
Valve seat
Spring
Valve body
O-rings

Ball faucet tool

1 Turn off the hot and cold water at the stop valves and open the faucet to let any water drain from the pipes. Plug the sink drain with a towel to avoid losing small parts. Pry off a red and blue hot/cold button or a knob-handle button, if present, with a small screwdriver or dull knife. Loosen the setscrew hidden underneath with the hex wrench on the ball faucet tool. Now remove the handle.

The ball-type faucet is used by Delta, Peerless, and a few others. The ball fits into the faucet body and is constructed with three holes (not visible here)— a hot inlet, a cold inlet, and the outlet, which fills the valve body with water that then flows to the spout or sprayer. Depending on the position of the ball, each inlet hole is open, closed, or somewhere in-between. The inlet holes are sealed to the ball with valve seats, which are pressed tight against the ball with springs. If water drips from the spout, replace the seats and springs. Or go ahead and purchase an entire replacement kit and replace all or most of the working parts.

Faceted edge

2 Wrap the jaws of your channel-type pliers with masking tape to protect the faucet finish. Grasp the faceted or knurled edges of the round ball cap with the pliers and twist to remove.

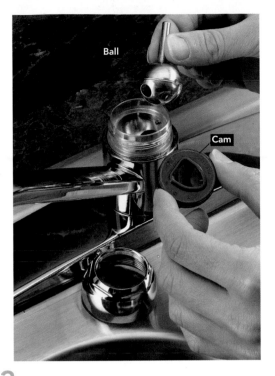

3 Pull out the ball, noticing for later how a pin in the faucet body fits in a slit in the ball. Clean the ball with white vinegar and a toothbrush or replace it if it is scratched.

4 If your faucet drips from the spout, it's because the seal between the ball and the hot- or cold-water intake has failed. Pull the neoprene valve seats and springs from the intakes with a screwdriver. Note how the cupped sides of the valve seats fit over the narrow sides of the springs and how the wide base of the springs fit into holes in the intakes.

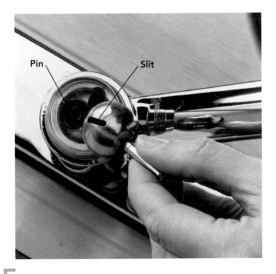

5 Replace parts in the reverse order they came off. Each spring/seat washer combo can be lined up on a screwdriver, set in place, and pushed in with a finger. The pin in the faucet body fits in a slit on the ball. The pointy side of the cam faces forward, and lugs on the sides of the cam fit in notches in the valve body.

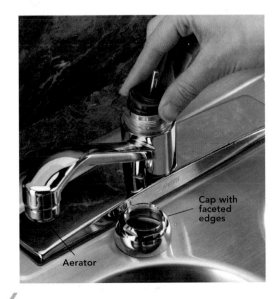

6 Make sure the adjusting ring is partly backed off before screwing the cap on. After the cap is on, gently tighten down the adjusting ring with the ball faucet tool. Remove the aerator, turn on the water supply and test. If water leaks from under the handle or if the handle action is stiff, tighten or loosen the adjusting ring. Replace the aerator.

HOW TO FIX A DISC FAUCET

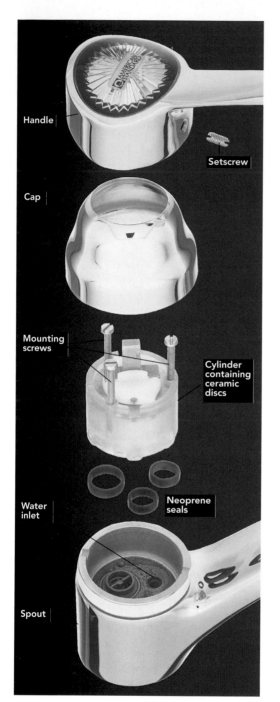

Handle

Setscrew

Cap

Mounting screws

Cylinder containing ceramic discs

Water inlet

Neoprene seals

Spout

The disc-type faucet used by American Standard, among others, has a wide disc cartridge hidden beneath the handle and the cap. Mounting screws hold the cartridge in the valve body. Two tight-fitting ceramic discs with holes in them are concealed inside the cartridge. The handle slides the top disc back and forth and from side to side over the stationary bottom disc. This brings the holes in the disks into and out of alignment, adjusting the flow and mix of hot and cold water.

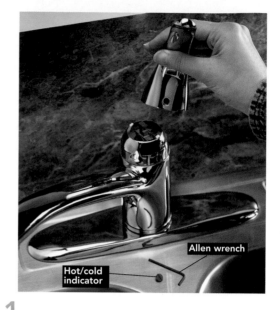

Allen wrench

Hot/cold indicator

1 Turn off the hot and cold water at the stop valves, open the faucet to let any water drain out, and plug the sink drain. Pry the index cap (and possibly a hot/cold indicator) off the handle with a small screwdriver or a dull knife. Loosen the handle setscrew with a Phillips or slotted screwdriver or an Allen wrench and remove the handle.

Cylinder containing ceramic discs

Cap

Retaining screws

2 Remove the chrome cap and/or a plastic or metal retaining ring with channel-type pliers (cover the jaws with masking tape). Remove the cylinder containing the discs, generally by first removing three long retaining screws. Take time to line up parts in the orientation and order in which they were installed.

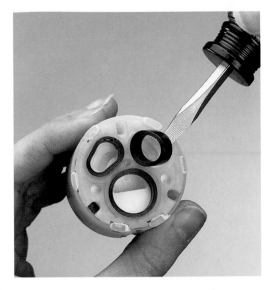

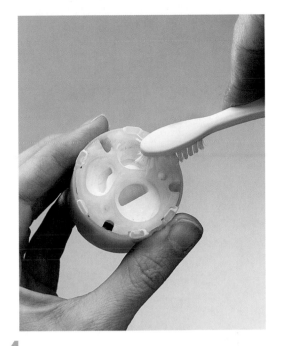

3 If your faucet leaks under the handle, remove the three neoprene seals from the underside of the disc cylinder. Bring them to the hardware store and find matching replacements. For a leak out of the spout, you need to replace the entire cylinder.

4 If you are reusing the cylinder, clean the water inlets, scouring with a toothbrush and white vinegar if they are crusty.

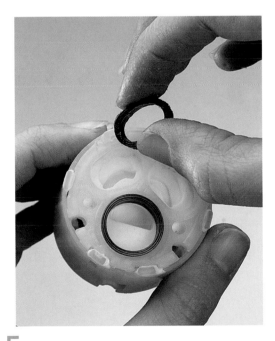

5 Lightly coat the new neoprene seals with heatproof grease and insert them in the appropriate openings in the cylinder. The seals will be slippery and you'll need to contort them a bit to fit the shapes of the openings, so be sure to do this over a clean, light colored surface so you don't lose the seals.

6 Insert the cylinder and secure it to the faucet body with the cylinder screws. Reattach the retaining nut. Reattach the handle, then turn on the hot and cold supplies and test the faucet. Remove the aerator from the spout to allow debris to escape.

My Bathroom Sink Drains Slowly

5

If your bathroom sink drains slowly, or not at all, the plug is most likely right under the pop-up stopper.

HAIR, SOAP, SOAPY HAIR, HAIRY SOAP—there are any number of things that can plug up a bathroom sink drain, but a couple of materials seem to show up a lot. Hair likes to tangle on the shaft of the pop up stopper, and soap likes to join in the fun by congealing on the hair. Eventually, you can get a long icky rope that snakes down into the trap. So the first thing is to figure out how to remove the pop-up stopper. While you're at it, withdraw the horizontal pivot arm that actuates the stopper. Nine times out of ten, you can vanquish the soap rope by removing and cleaning these two snags. A plunger can flush the beast from a deeper lair. Or you can remove that bend of pipe under the sink called the trap and give this a good cleaning. Finally, with a miraculous tool called an auger, you can pursue the soap rope beyond the trap into the dark and mysterious reaches of your drainage system.

In the event that your pop-up stopper drain needs replacement, see pages 126 to 129.

POP-UP STOPPERS 101

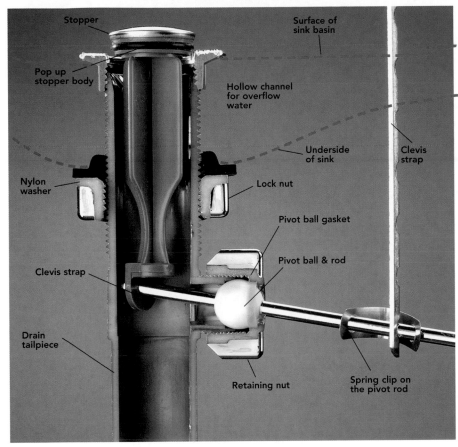

Stopper

Surface of sink basin

Pop up stopper body

Hollow channel for overflow water

Underside of sink

Clevis strap

Nylon washer

Lock nut

Pivot ball gasket

Pivot ball & rod

Clevis strap

Drain tailpiece

Retaining nut

Spring clip on the pivot rod

Pop-up stoppers keep objects from falling down the drain, and they make filling and draining the sink easy. They also accumulate hair and soap and require periodic cleaning. Cleaning the pop-up stopper provides an opportunity to adjust the actuating mechanism so the stopper works better.

TERMS YOU NEED TO KNOW

POP-UP STOPPER—the drain stopper and the shaft attached to the bottom of the stopper.

PIVOT BALL & ROD—The ball is a fulcrum and the rod a lever, which allows the pop-up stopper to be moved up and down.

TAILPIECE—takes the waste from the pop-up-stopper body to the trap.

TRAP—a bend of drainpipe below the sink. It's always full of water to keep sewer gases from rising into the house.

TRAP ARM—receives waste from the trap and takes it to the fixture drain line in the wall.

FIXTURE DRAIN LINE—begins at the wall and eventually joins with larger drain pipes. On older houses, the drain line may come vertically from the floor.

TOOLS & SUPPLIES YOU'LL NEED

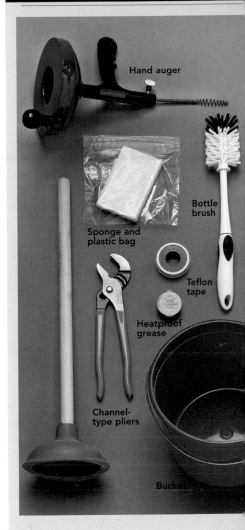

Hand auger

Bottle brush

Sponge and plastic bag

Teflon tape

Heatproof grease

Channel-type pliers

Bucket

SKILLS YOU'LL NEED

• Making pipe connections

• Using plungers

• Auger cranking

DIFFICULTY LEVEL

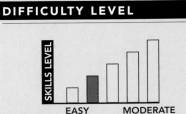

SKILLS LEVEL

EASY   MODERATE

Time: about 1 hour

HOW TO CLEAN A POP-UP STOPPER

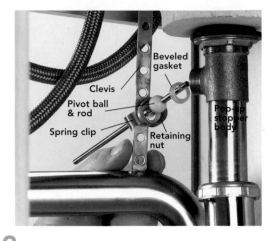

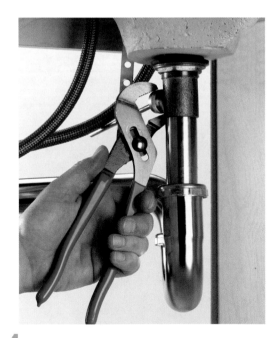

1 If the bathroom sink drain is clogged, first bail most of the water out of the sink. Remove the pop-up stopper, noticing as you do how its shaft was oriented in the sink. To remove, try rotating the stopper a quarter turn while tilting the shaft of the stopper away from the pivot arm. If it cannot be freed through gentle manipulation, proceed to step 2.

2 Put a bucket under the drain works. Unscrew the retaining nut attached to the drain tailpiece. Remove the pivot ball and rod, the beveled gasket that seals the ball, and any other washers. You may need to squeeze a spring clip on the pivot rod to move the rod in the clevis.

3 Clean the gunk off the pop-up stopper and rod with hot soapy water and a brush. Clear accessible parts of the drain hole with a long screwdriver or a bottlebrush. Temporarily put the washers, the ball and rod, and the nut back on, but leave the stopper off. Run hot tap water down the drain. If the sink won't drain, plunge as described on the next page.

4 Once the water is draining well, remove and replace the pop-up assembly pieces in the correct order. Apply pipe joint compound to the inside of the pop-up stopper body where the beveled washer sits, and onto the threads that receive the retaining nut. The pivot rod must penetrate a hole at the bottom of the pop-up stopper shaft, which is put in before or after the rod, depending on your faucet model.

HOW TO PLUNGE A BATHROOM SINK

1 Plunging a plugged bathroom sink is usually the next step after cleaning the pop up mechanism. Be prepared to get the bathroom and yourself wet. The stopper should be removed and the pivot ball in place (see previous page). Put a wet sponge in a plastic bag and stuff this in the overflow opening. You may need to have somebody hold this in place while you plunge.

2 Put enough water in the sink to cover the plunger. Rhythmically thrust the plunger up and down with an occasional extra hard thrust up or down. It can take a bit of work. When you've cleared the drain, pour a large pot of boiling water down the drain and follow that with hot tap water. If the plunging doesn't work, remove and clean the trap (see page 42). If the clog wasn't in the trap, follow the steps on the following pages to auger the waste line beyond the trap.

TOOL TIP

The standard redheaded plunger seen in step 2 is the most commonly used plunger for sinks, but the flare-cup style plunger seen here also works. All you need to do is fold the flaps on the working end of the plunger up into the plunger head to create a flat bottom capable of producing ample suction for clearing a sink.

SINK DRAIN MAINTENANCE

Pour a large pot of boiling water down your bathroom sink every so often. Very hot water melts soap better than just about anything.

HOW TO CLEAN A SINK DRAIN TRAP

HOW TO CLEAR A FIXTURE DRAIN LINE WITH AN AUGER

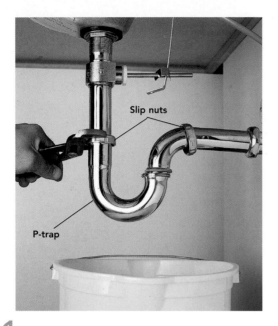

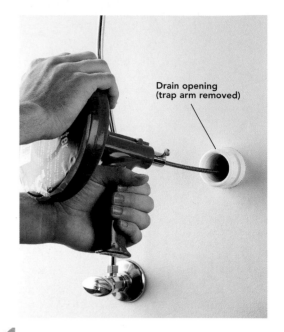

Drain opening
(trap arm removed)

1 Position a bucket under the trap to catch water and debris. Loosen the slip nuts on the trap bend with channel-type pliers. Unscrew the nuts, slide them away from the connections, and pull off the trap bend.

1 A hand auger (often called a snake) is used to clear clogs in drain lines when they occur after the trap. To access the drain line, remove the trap arm and push the end of the auger cable into the drain line opening until resistance is met. This resistance usually indicates that the cable has reached a bend in the drain line.

2 Empty the trap into the bucket and use a small wire brush or a bottlebrush to ream out and clean the trap. Soak the trap in very hot water to dissolve and remove any blockages from soap buildup. Reassemble the trap.

2 Set the auger lock so that at least 6" of cable extends out of the opening. Crank the auger handle in a clockwise direction to move the end of the cable past the bend in the drain line.

3 Release the lock and continue pushing the cable into the opening until firm resistance is felt. Set the auger lock and crank the handle in a clockwise direction. Solid resistance that prevents the cable from advancing indicates a clog. Some clogs, such as a sponge or an accumulation of hair, can be snagged and retrieved. Continuous resistance that still allows the cable to advance at a very slow rate is probably a soap clog.

RETRIEVAL OPTION: Pull an obstruction out of the line by releasing the auger lock and cranking the handle counter-clockwise while manually feeding the cable back into the auger drum. Removing the whole obstruction may take a number of tries. Call a plumber or go to "Advanced clog cleaning" pages 80 to 81 if the clog can't be cleared.

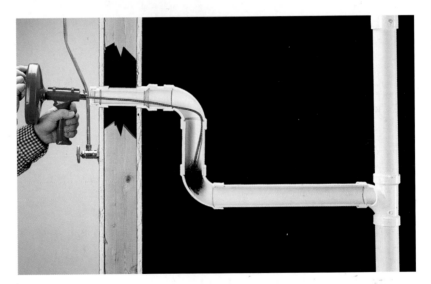

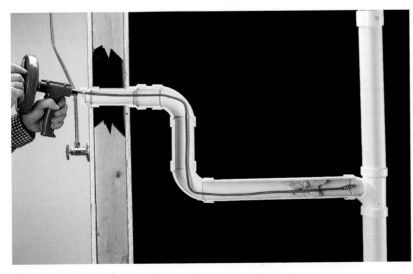

BREAK APART OPTION: Built-up clogs (as opposed to objects) can be broken into small pieces with the auger head and then flushed from the system. Bore through the clog by cranking the handle clockwise while applying steady pressure on the hand grip of the auger. Repeat the procedure two or three times, then reel in the cable. Reconnect the trap and flush the line with boiling hot water.

My Water Pressure is Low or Uneven

6

Restoring vigorous water pressure to your water outlets can be as simple as cleaning a filter in a faucet or showerhead.

CORRECTING LOW WATER PRESSURE AT A SINK OR SHOWER MAY BE EASIER THAN YOU'D EXPECT. Minerals and rust can collect in the finely perforated screens and sprayers in sink spouts and showerheads. Clean these out and, voilà, the water flows with vigor; no plumber needed. Before water reaches any fixture or appliance, it passes through a shutoff valve or two. Make sure these are fully open. Washing machines also draw water through filters. Clean these screens and your washer may fill faster. Old iron water pipes are subject to mineral buildup. A professional can replace these with modern copper or plastic pipes that resist buildup and corrosion.

WATER FLOW 101

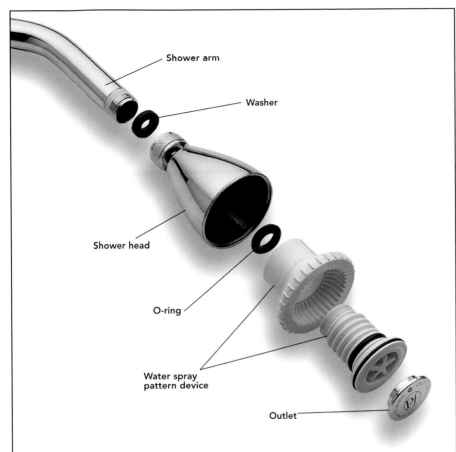

Shower arm

Washer

Shower head

O-ring

Water spray
pattern device

Outlet

A showerhead is easy to remove for cleaning or repair. Once you remove it from the shower arm, you take it apart, clean the parts (you may need to check the flow restrictor), and then reassemble it and reattach it to the arm.

TERMS YOU NEED TO KNOW

AERATOR—a small cylinder on the end of a bathroom or kitchen sink spout that breaks up the water stream so it doesn't splash.

FLOW RESTRICTOR—a disc-shaped part on the inlet side of a showerhead with a small hole or holes designed to restrict water flow and conserve water.

TOOLS & SUPPLIES YOU'LL NEED

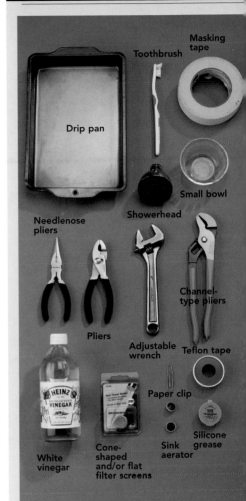

Masking tape

Toothbrush

Drip pan

Small bowl

Showerhead

Needlenose pliers

Channel-type pliers

Pliers

Adjustable wrench

Teflon tape

Paper clip

White vinegar

Cone-shaped and/or flat filter screens

Sink aerator

Silicone grease

SKILLS YOU'LL NEED

• Using channel-type pliers

• Using a wrench

DIFFICULTY LEVEL

SKILLS LEVEL

EASY   MODERATE

Time: less than ½ hour per fixture

HOW TO CLEAN A SHOWERHEAD

THE FIRST SPOT TO CHECK

Water may flow through two or three shut-off valves between the city water line or the well and your shower or sink. Make sure all the shutoff valves are functioning properly and are opened fully. If the valves are all open, the problem could be in the internal working of your outlet valves. Check the filters and aerators first, as we show you in this project. If the water flow is still subpar, refer to the project that show you how to repair and replace faucets.

1 Remove the showerhead from the shower arm by unscrewing the collar nut that houses the swivel ball and is threaded onto the shower arm. You may need to grip the shower arm with channel-type pliers to keep it from twisting. Wrap the jaws of the pliers with masking tape to protect shower parts.

2 Once the showerhead is fully removed, run water through the shower arm for a couple of minutes to clear it.

3 Disassemble the showerhead. On newer showerheads, the swivel ball or the inlet side of the showerhead will have flow restriction parts. These contain one or more small holes and exist mainly to conserve water. Remove these parts, if you can, with a small knife or screwdriver.

4 Keep all parts in order and oriented in the correct up/down position. If the house water pressure is very poor, you may leave the flow restriction parts (inset photo) out when you put the showerhead back together. WARNING: Removing flow restrictor parts can dramatically increase your water and energy bills.

5 Use a paper clip or pin to clean the outlet holes on the showerhead then flush all parts clean with water. Soak encrusted parts overnight in white vinegar to soften mineral deposits.

6 Coat the rubber O-ring that contacts the swivel ball with silicone grease before reassembling the head. Hand-tighten the collar nut that holds the swivel fitting to the showerhead.

7 Wrap the shower arm threads with two or three layers of Teflon tape in a clockwise direction before replacing the head. Tighten the head to the shower arm a little more than hand tight using your adjustable wrench. Tighten a little more if the joint drips with the shower on. If the showerhead does not work to your satisfaction, replace it.

HOW TO CLEAN A FAUCET AERATOR

1 Dry and wrap the aerator with masking tape to protect the finish. Adjust channel-type pliers to fit comfortably over the aerator and twist the aerator counterclockwise to loosen.

2 Finish unscrewing the aerator by hand then gently prod apart its components with your finger or a needle or other pointed tool. Be careful to lay out pieces in the order they fit together and in the correct up/down orientation. TIP: Turn on the water while the aerator is removed to flush any built-up materials out the spout.

3 Clean parts with white vinegar and a toothbrush. Soften mineral deposits by soaking overnight in the vinegar. Replace the aerator at a hardware store or home center if parts are damaged or difficult to clean. A standard replacement aerator has both male and female threads and fits most faucets, but take in your old aerator in case yours is a non-standard size.

4 Reassemble the aerator exactly as it came apart and hand-tighten it onto the spout. Remove the tape. Replace the aerator if it still doesn't work right.

WASHING MACHINE FILLS SLOWLY?

1 Turn off hot and cold water to the machine and unscrew supply hoses where they join the machine or at the first accessible coupling.

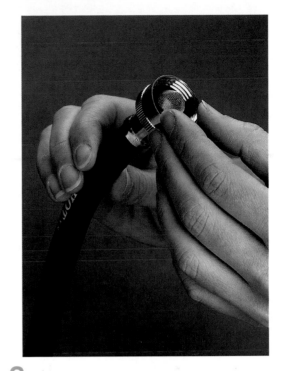

2 Some water supply hoses for washing machines contain filter screens in the hose couplings that connect to the water supply and to the water inlets in the washing machine. If you find these filters, carefully remove and clean them.

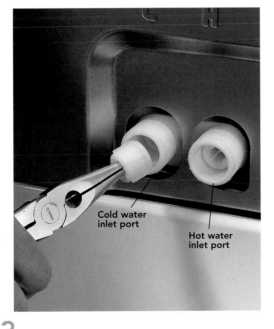

Cold water
inlet port

Hot water
inlet port

3 Most washing machines contain filter screens at the water inlet port. Remove the cone filter with needlenose pliers and clear debris from the filter screen. If the filter is in poor condition, replace it.

4 Apply Teflon tape to the male pipe threads at the water inlet connection and retighten all hoses.

Runaway Toilet

7

Jiggling the handle can make a running toilet stop, but it's only a temporary solution. Making real repairs is a lot easier than you might think.

SNORING, TICKING CLOCKS, DRIPPING FAUCETS, AND RUNNING TOILETS are perhaps the four greatest nighttime annoyances. Together they conspire to keep you from the blissful slumber you deserve. For help on fixing leaky faucets, see pages 28 to 37. If your toilet runs and runs and you just can't seem to catch up with it, you're in the right place. This project will show you how to diagnose and remedy the most common causes for the perpetually running toilet.

TOILET TROUBLE SHOOTING 101

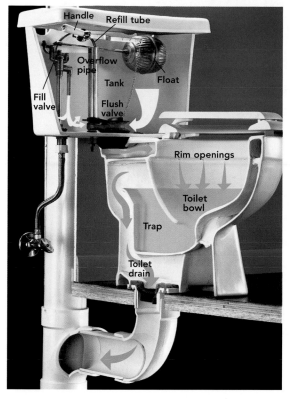

Labels on the diagram: Handle, Refill tube, Overflow pipe, Tank, Float, Fill valve, Flush valve, Rim openings, Toilet bowl, Trap, Toilet drain

Five steps of a perfect flush: 1. The *handle* opens the *flush valve*, emptying the *tank* into the *toilet bowl*. 2. Water races through *rim openings* and the *siphon jet* at the base of the bowl. 3. The sudden surge causes the water to exit the *trap* and bowl as a unit, siphoning itself down the *toilet drain*. 4. The *ballcock* (fill valve) opens when the *float* drops to refill the tank. The *refill tube* directs some of the water down the *overflow pipe* to refill the bowl. 5. The *float* turns off the *fill valve* when enough water has entered the *tank*.

Most toilets can be fixed with generic replacement parts. However, some brands require special parts, especially newer models, which may have larger flush valves. Contact your manufacturer (see page 140 for a list) or go to a well-equipped plumbing-supply house. Identify your toilet brand, which is often written behind (not on) the seat, and its model number (usually stamped inside the tank or tank lid). Always bring old parts with you to the store for reference.

TERMS YOU NEED TO KNOW

BALLCOCK/FILL VALVE—These terms both refer to the valve that fills the tank after you flush the toilet. Traditionally, the ballcock is turned on and off by a float ball on a rod. Modern cup-float fill valves can be used to replace most old ball-cocks.

FLUSH VALVE—the assembly that releases water from the tank into the bowl when the toilet is flushed. It includes the overflow pipe, the valve seat (hole), and the flapper or tank ball that covers the hole. Universal flapper-style flush valves can replace old tank ball or flapper flush valves on most toilets.

STOP VALVE—the valve that turns off water to the toilet. Turn to page 105 to replace.

SUPPLY—the hose or tube that takes water from the stop valve to the tank.

Turn to page 105 to replace.

TOOLS & SUPPLIES YOU'LL NEED

Labels: Soft cloth, Bucket, Screwdriver, Tape measure, Adjustable wrench, Teflon tape, Scissors, Bullet level, Needle-nose pliers, Pliers, Hacksaw, Screwdriver, Float cup fill valve, Flush valve with a flapper, Flashlight, Large sponge, Channel-type pliers

SKILLS YOU'LL NEED

• Patience

• Observation

• Willingness to call a manufacturer help center if you get into trouble

DIFFICULTY LEVEL

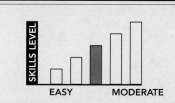

SKILLS LEVEL

EASY   MODERATE

Time: 5 minutes or hours depending on problem

HOW TO RESET TANK WATER LEVEL

1 Perhaps the most common cause of running toilets is a minor misadjustment that fails to tell the water to shut off when the toilet tank is full. The culprit is usually a float ball or cup that is adjusted to set a water level in the tank that's higher than the top of the overflow pipe, which serves as a drain for excess tank water.

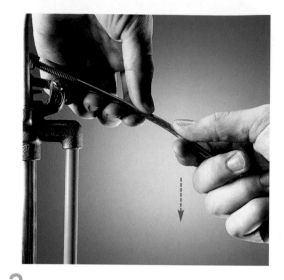

2 A ball float is connected to a float arm that's attached to a plunger on the other end. As the tank fills, the float rises and lifts one end of the float arm. At a certain point, the float arm depresses the plunger and stops the flow of water. By simply bending the float arm downward a bit you can cause it to depress the plunger at a lower tank water level, solving the problem.

Spring clip

3 A diaphragm fill valve usually is made of plastic and has a wide bonnet that contains a rubber diaphragm. Turn the adjustment screw clockwise to lower the water level and counter-clockwise to raise it.

4 A float cup fill valve is made of plastic and is easy to adjust. Lower the water level by pinching the spring clip with fingers or pliers and moving the clip and cup down the pull rod and shank. Raise the water level by moving the clip and cup upward.

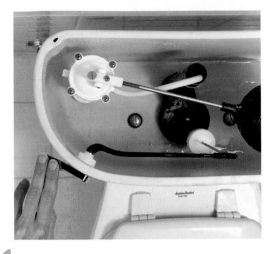

1 Sometimes there is plenty of water in the tank, but not enough of it makes it to the bowl before the flush valve shuts off the water from the tank. Modern toilets are designed to leave some water in the tank, since the first water that leaves the tank does so with the most force. (It's pressed out by the weight of the water on top). To increase the duration of the flush, shorten the length of the chain between the flapper and the float (yellow in the model shown).

2 The handle lever should pull straight up on the flapper. If it doesn't, reposition the chain hook on the handle lever. When the flapper is covering the opening, there should be just a little slack in the chain. If there is too much slack, shorten the chain and cut off excess with the cutters on your pliers. Turn the water back on at the stop valve and test the flush.

3 If the toilet is not completing flushes and the lever and chain for the flapper or tank ball are correctly adjusted, the problem could be that the handle mechanism needs cleaning or replacement. Remove the chain/linkage from the handle lever. Remove the nut on the backside of the handle with an adjustable wrench. It unthreads clockwise (the reverse of standard nuts). Remove the old handle from the tank.

4 Unless the handle parts are visibly broken, try cleaning them with an old toothbrush dipped in white vinegar. Replace the handle and test the action. If it sticks or is hard to operate, replace it. Most replacement handles come with detailed instructions that tell you how to install and adjust them.

HOW TO REPLACE A FILL VALVE

1 Toilet fill valves degrade eventually and need to be replaced. Before removing the old fill valve, shut off the water supply at the fixture stop valve located on the tube that supplies water to the tank. Flush the toilet and sponge out the remaining water. Then, remove the old fill valve assembly by loosening and removing the mounting nut on the outside of the tank wall that secures the fill valve.

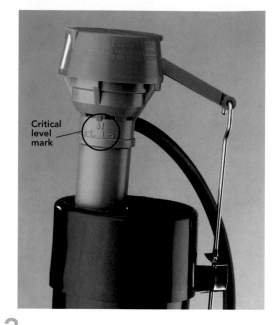

Critical level mark

2 Fill valves need to be coordinated with the flush valve so the tank water level is not higher than the overflow pipe and so the fill valve is not low enough in the tank that it creates a siphoning hazard. New fill valves have a "critical level" mark ("CL") near the top of the valve.

3 The new fill valve must be installed so the Critical Level ("CL") mark is at least 1" above the overflow pipe. Slip the shank washer on the threaded shank of the new fill valve and place the valve in the hole so the washer is flat on the tank bottom. Compare the locations of the CL mark and the overflow pipe.

4 Adjust the height of the fill valve shank so the "CL" line and overflow pipe will be correctly related. Different products are adjusted in different ways—the fill valve shown here telescopes when it's twisted.

Threaded valve stem

5 Position the valve in the tank. Push down on the valve shank (not the top) while hand tightening the locknut onto the threaded valve stem (thread the mounting nut on the exterior side of tank). Hand-tighten only.

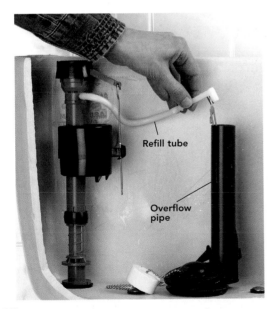

Refill tube

Overflow pipe

7 If the overflow pipe has a cap, remove it. Attach one end of the refill tube from the new valve to the plastic angle adapter and the other end to the refill nipple near the top of the valve. Attach the angle adapter to the overflow pipe. Cut off excess tubing with scissors to prevent kinking. WARNING: Don't insert the refill tube into the overflow pipe. The outlet of the refill tube needs to be above the top of pipe for it to work properly.

6 Hook up the water by attaching the coupling nut from the supply riser to the threaded shank at the bottom end of the new fill valve. Hand-tighten only.

8 Turn the water on fully. Slightly tighten any fitting that drips water. Adjust the water level in the tank by squeezing the spring clip on the float cup with needlenose pliers and moving the cup up or down on the link bar. Test the flush.

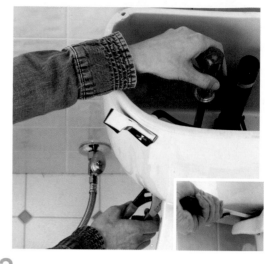

1 If the fixes on the previous pages still do not stop your toilet from running, the next step it to try replacing the flush valve. Before removing the old flush valve, shut off the water supply at the fixture stop valve located on the tube that supplies water to the tank. Flush the toilet and sponge out the remaining water. To make this repair you'll need to remove the tank from the bowl. Start by unscrewing the water supply coupling nut from the bottom of the tank.

2 Unscrew the bolts holding the toilet tank to the bowl by loosening the nuts from below. If you are having difficulty unscrewing the tank bolts and nuts because they are fused together by rust or corrosion, apply penetrating oil or spray lubricant to the threads, give it a few minutes to penetrate and then try again. If that fails, slip an open-ended hacksaw (or plain hacksaw blade) between the tank and bowl and saw through the bolt (inset photo).

3 Unhook the chain from the handle lever arm. Remove the tank and carefully place it upside-down on an old towel. Remove the spud washer and spud nut from the base of the flush valve using a spud wrench or large channel-type pliers. Remove the old flush valve.

4 Place the new flush valve in the valve hole and check to see if the top of the overflow pipe is at least 1" below the Critical Level line (see page 54) and the tank opening where the handle is installed. If the pipe is too tall, cut it to length with a hacksaw.

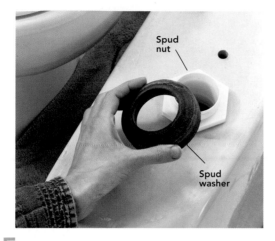

5 Position the flush valve flapper below the handle lever arm and secure it to the tank from beneath with the spud nut. Tighten the nut one-half turn past hand tight with a spud wrench or large channel-type pliers. Over tightening may cause the tank to break. Put the new spud washer over the spud nut, small side down.

6 With the tank lying on its back, thread a rubber washer onto each tank bolt and insert it into the bolt holes from inside the tank. Then, thread a brass washer and hex nut onto the tank bolts from below and tighten them to a quarter turn past hand tight. Do not overtighten.

7 With the hex nuts tightened against the tank bottom, carefully lower the tank over the bowl and set it down so the spud washer seats neatly over the water inlet in the bowl and the tank bolts fit through the holes in the bowl flange. Secure the tank to the bowl with a rubber washer, brass washer, and nut or wing nut at each bolt end. Press the tank to level as you hand-tighten the nuts. Hook up the water supply at the fill valve inlet.

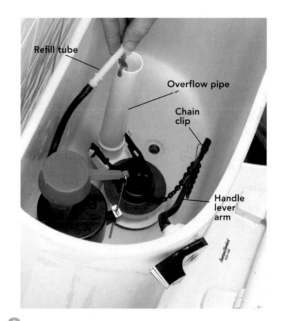

8 Connect the chain clip to the handle lever arm and adjust the number of links to allow for a little slack in the chain when the flapper is closed. Leave a little tail on the chain for adjusting, cutting off remaining excess. Attach the refill tube to the top of the overflow pipe the same way it had been attached to the previous refill pipe. Turn on the water supply at the stop valve and test the flush. (Some flush valve flappers are adjustable.)

Toilet Clogged. Overflowing!

8

A blockage in the toilet bowl leaves flush water from the tank nowhere to go but on the floor.

THE TOILET IS CLOGGED AND HAS OVERFLOWED, or perhaps its gorge has simply risen, lapped the canyon walls but not yet topped the rim. Have patience. Now is the time for considered action. A second flush is a tempting but unnecessary gamble. First, do damage control. Mop up the water if there's been a spill. Next, consider the nature of the clog. Is it entirely "natural" or might a foreign object be contributing to the congestion? Push a natural blockage down the drain with a plunger. A foreign object should be removed, if possible, with a closet auger. Pushing anything more durable than toilet paper into the sewer may create a more serious blockage in your drain and waste system. If the tub, sink, and toilet all become clogged at once, the branch drainline that serves all the bathroom fixtures is probably blocked and your best recourse is to call a drain clearing service.

CLOGGED TOILETS 101

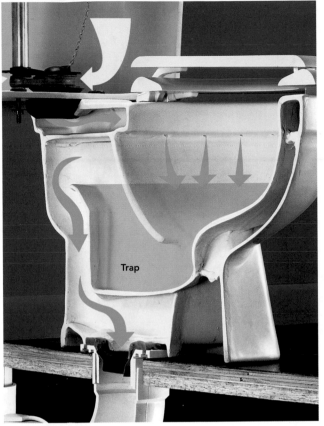

Trap

Towels

Plunger with
foldout skirt
(force cup)

Closet auger

The *trap* is the most common catching spot for toilet clogs, Once the clog forms, flushing the toilet cannot generate enough water power to clear the trap, so flush water backs up. Traps on modern 1.6-gallon toilets have been redesigned to larger diameters and are less prone to clogs than the first generation of 1.6 gal-lon toilets.

Not all plungers were created equal. The *standard plunger* (left) is simply an inverted rubber cup and is used to plunge sinks, tubs, and showers. The *flanged plunger,* also called a *force cup*, is designed to get down into the trap of a toilet drain. But in a pinch you can fold the flange up into the flanged plunger cup and use it as a standard plunger.

SKILLS YOU'LL NEED

- Vigorous plunging
- Using a closet auger

TERMS YOU NEED TO KNOW

WATER SEAL—Because of the loop-like shape of a toilet's plumbing, there is always water in the bowl and in the passage directly behind the bowl. This water seal keeps sewer gases from rising into the house.

TOILET TRAP—A "trap" in plumbing refers to a bend that holds a water seal, so technically, the toilet bowl is part of the trap. But usually people are talking about the back, hidden portion of that bend when they speak of the toilet trap.

FLUSH VALVE—is the flapper covering the hole in the bottom of the tank that sits behind the bowl. The toilet flushes when this is opened.

CONTROLLED FLUSH—the letting of water from the tank to bowl by manually lifting and closing the flush valve. This prevents bowl overflow when you're not sure the clog is gone.

DIFFICULTY LEVEL

SKILLS LEVEL

EASY   MODERATE

Time: 15 to 30 minutes

HOW TO PLUNGE A CLOGGED TOILET

A flanged plunger fits into the mouth of the toilet trap and creates a tight seal so you can build up enough pressure in front of the plunger to dislodge the blockage and send it on its way.

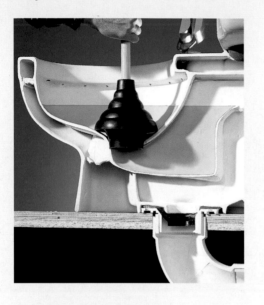

1 Plunging is the easiest way to remove "natural" blockages. Take time to lay towels around the base of the toilet and remove other objects to a safe, dry location, since plunging may result in splashing. Sometimes, allowing a very full toilet to sit for twenty or thirty minutes will permit some of the water to drain to a less precarious level, or you can bail it out. **WARNING:** Don't use a plunger if the toilet is plugged with a diaper, washcloth, or other object that could get pushed into the drainpipe. It may create a worse clog in a pipe that's beyond your reach. Try to remove the object with a closet auger.

2 There should be enough water in the bowl to completely cover the plunger. Fold out the skirt from inside the plunger to form a better seal with the opening at the base of the bowl. Pump the plunger vigorously half-a-dozen times, take a rest, and then repeat. Try this for 10 to 15 cycles.

3 If you force enough water out of the bowl that you are unable to create suction with the plunger, put a controlled amount of water in the bowl by lifting up on the flush valve in the tank. Resume plunging. When you think the drain is clear, you can try a controlled flush, with your hand ready to close the flush valve should the water threaten to spill out of the bowl. Once the blockage has cleared, dump a five-gallon pail of water into the toilet to blast away any residual debris.

HOW TO CLEAR CLOGS WITH A CLOSET AUGER

TOOL TIP

A closet auger is a semirigid cable housed in a tube. The tube has a bend at the end so it can be snaked through a toilet trap (without scratching it) to snag blockages.

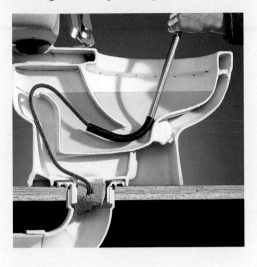

Protective rubber boot

1 Place the business end of the auger firmly in the bottom of the toilet bowl with the auger tip fully withdrawn. A rubber sleeve will protect the porcelain at the bottom bend of the auger. The tip will be facing back and up, which is the direction the toilet trap takes.

2 Rotate the handle on the auger housing clockwise as you push down on the rod, advancing the rotating auger tip up into the back part of the trap. You may work the cable backward and forward as needed, but keep the rubber boot of the auger firmly in place in the bowl. When you feel resistance, indicating you've snagged the object, continue rotating the auger counterclockwise as you withdraw the cable and the object.

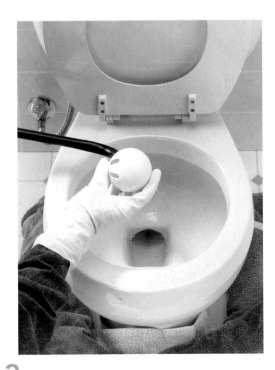

3 Fully retract the auger until you have recovered the object. This can be frustrating at times, but it is still a much easier task than the alternative—to remove the toilet and go fishing.

Fixing a Leaky Tub & Shower

9

Tub/shower plumbing is notorious for developing drips from the tub spout and the showerhead. In most cases, the leak can be traced to the valves controlled by the faucet handles.

DOES YOUR TUB/SHOWER DRIP, DRIP, DRIP from the spout or the showerhead even when the water is turned off? Chances are, a washer or cartridge in the faucet valve needs attention or replacement. But these parts vary widely by type and by brand name. The most critical part of a good repair job does not involve wrenches and screwdrivers, but the telephone and possibly a computer. That's because finding the brand name, model number, and ultimately part numbers will let you get the exact materials you'll need to do the job right. From there, it's a pretty easy repair.

TUB & SHOWER FAUCETS 101

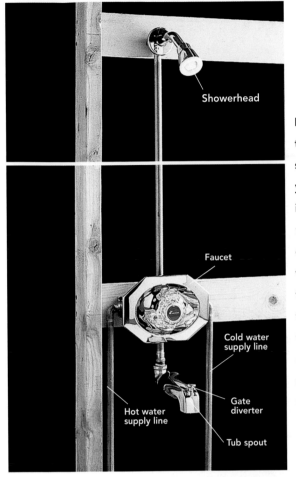

Showerhead

Faucet

Cold water
supply line

Hot water
supply line

Gate
diverter

Tub spout

If you could make your tub/shower and the tub surround above it disappear, you'd see pipes and plumbing parts similar to this. The *faucet* seen here only has one handle that controls the water volume and temperature. The water is directed to either the *tub spout* or the *showerhead* with a *diverter* located in the tub spout. Some two-handle models are joined by a third handle that serves as a diverter instead of the gate on the spout.

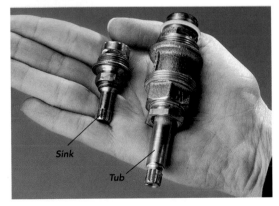

As the stem assemblies (right) demonstrate, sink and tub compression valves share the same genetics but vary in size and the particulars.

Sink

Tub

TERMS YOU NEED TO KNOW

COMPRESSION FAUCET—a two-or three-handle faucet that uses a simple stem and washer compression valve.

CARTRIDGE FAUCET—a one-, two-, or three-handle faucet with a valve or valves that uses a narrow, cylinder-shaped cartridge, which is moved in the valve body by the handle to channel hot and cold water.

TOOLS & SUPPLIES YOU'LL NEED

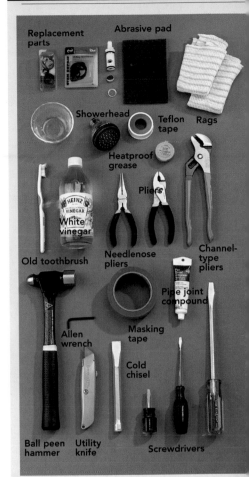

Replacement parts

Abrasive pad

Showerhead

Teflon tape

Rags

Heatproof grease

White vinegar

Pliers

Old toothbrush

Needlenose pliers

Channel-type pliers

Pipe joint compound

Allen wrench

Masking tape

Cold chisel

Ball peen hammer

Utility knife

Screwdrivers

SKILLS YOU'LL NEED

- Using channel-type pliers
- Tracking the order and arrangement of parts
- Phone or computer research

DIFFICULTY LEVEL

SKILLS LEVEL

EASY   MODERATE

Time: 1 hour plus research and shopping

HOW TO FIX A LEAKY ONE-HANDLE FAUCET

Water supply line to showerhead

Built-in shutoff valves

Hot water supply line

Control valve

Cold water supply line

Escutcheon

Gate diverter

1 Single-handle tub and shower faucets have one valve controlling both hot and cold water. This valve sits directly behind the one large knob or lever. If your tub spout drips all the time, you need to fix this valve. The first step involves information and materials gathering (see "Steps to Successful Shopping" on page 67). Next, turn off the hot and cold water supplies. Make sure the diverter is in the tub-filling position, then drain residual water out of the plumbing by opening the faucet to hot and cold water. Lay towels in the tub to prevent damaging the finish with tools and losing small parts.

2 Remove the handle of the damaged valve by first prying an index cap off the front with a dull knife or screwdriver and removing the screw hidden underneath. Pull off the handle. Remove any other parts obstructing the escutcheon, then remove the escutcheon. Keep parts in a safe place. Line them up and orient them as they sit in the faucet. If it's helpful, take digital pictures to remember how the parts went together.

3 Many one-handle tub and shower faucets have hot and cold shutoffs built in to the faucet body. Turn these off clockwise with a large slotted screwdriver. Integral stops are useful if you need to leave the water off for some time during a repair, and the only other turnoff to the tub and shower takes other fixtures out of commission. If you'd rather, you may turn off water at the nearest shutoff valves instead.

4 Remove the threaded retaining ring that secures the cartridge or stem and bonnet assembly (some models may use retaining screws to hold the stem). This unit is what turns the water on and controls the mix of hot and cold water.

5 Remove the cartridge, pulling gently on the stem with a pair of pliers if necessary. With the cartridge out, now is a good time to flush out the system by opening the shutoffs in the valve or in the supply line. Watch out, though, the water will come out of the valve opening, not the spout.

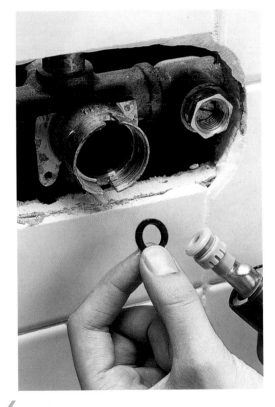

6 Clean the cartridge by flushing with warm water and replace the O-ring at the end (coat the new O-ring with heatproof grease). If the cartridge is old or visibly damaged, replace it. Reinstall the faucet parts in reverse order.

HOW TO FIX A LEAKY TWO- OR THREE-HANDLE FAUCET

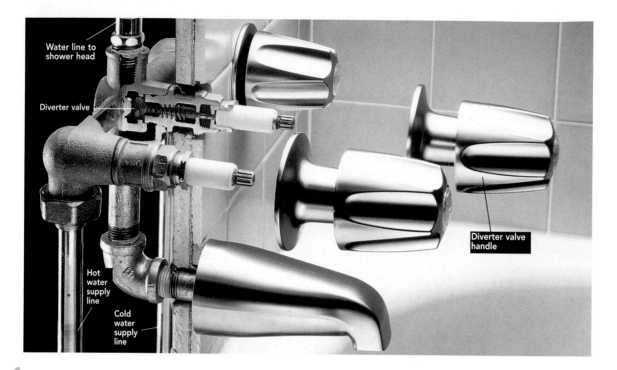

Water line to shower head

Diverter valve

Hot water supply line

Cold water supply line

Diverter valve handle

1 Both three-handle and two-handle faucets have a hot-water valve and a cold-water valve behind their hot and cold faucet handles. If water drips from the spout when the faucet is off, you need to determine which valve isn't working by shutting off the water supply on each line in turn at the shutoff valve. Two- and three-handle faucets are repaired in the same manner, except that the middle handle on the three-handle models is a diverter valve (the diverter on two-handle models is in the spout). If the showerhead on your three-handle system drips, or if you continue to get a high volume of water through the spout when it should be coming out the showerhead, it's the diverter handle that needs attention.

2 Determine which valve is causing the leak (see previous step) and remove the handle cover for that valve (in this case, the diverter valve is being worked upon). Also remove the escutcheon that covers the wall opening for that valve.

3 Remove the bonnet nut from the stem assembly using an adjustable wrench. If your faucet has cartridges, not compression valves as shown here, simply remove the cartridge (see p. 65).

4 Unscrew the stem assembly using a deep-set socket and a ratchet wrench. You may need to enlarge the opening in the wall slightly with a cold chisel and ball-peen hammer to gain clearance for the socket. TIP: You can purchase a shower valve socket wrench at most hardware stores. The most common sizes are $^{29}/_{32}$" and $^{31}/_{32}$".

5 Remove the brass stem screw from the compression valve. Find an exact match for the stem washer that's held in place by the stem screw. Disassemble the spindle and the valve retaining nut.

SHOPPING TIP

STEPS TO SUCCESSFUL SHOPPING

Identify the brand. This may be written on the faucet handle, on a plate behind the handle or handles, or elsewhere on the hardware of the tub or shower. Be aware that a name on a pop-up stopper, overflow cap, or showerhead may or may not be the manufacturer of your faucet.

Identify the model. The major brands have web sites and toll-free numbers. Use these to identify your model.

Identify replacement parts. It may be that all you will need for replacement parts are washers, screws, and a few common valve parts available at a well-equipped home center or hardware store. But if you need to replace a cartridge or other intricate faucet component, your manufacturer can provide parts numbers and tell you how to order these.

6 Clean the valve parts with white vinegar and a toothbrush or small wire brush. Coat all washers with heatproof grease and reassemble then reinstall the valve.

Bathtub or Shower Draining Poorly

10

As with bathroom sinks, tub and shower drain pipes may become clogged with soap and hair. The drain stopping mechanisms can also require cleaning and adjustment.

TUB OR SHOWER NOT DRAINING? First, make sure it's only the tub or shower. If your sink is plugged, too, it may be a coincidence or it may be that a common branch line is plugged. A sure sign of this is when water drains from the sink into the tub. This could require the help of a drain cleaning service, or a drum trap that services both the sink and tub needs cleaning. If the toilet also can't flush (or worse, water comes into the tub when you flush the toilet), then the common drain to all your bathroom fixtures is plugged. Call a drain cleaning service. If you suspect the problem is only with your tub or shower, then read on. We'll show you how to clear drainlines and clean and adjust two types of tub stopper mechanisms. Adjusting the mechanism can also help with the opposite problem: a tub that drains when you're trying to take a bath.

BATH DRAINS 101

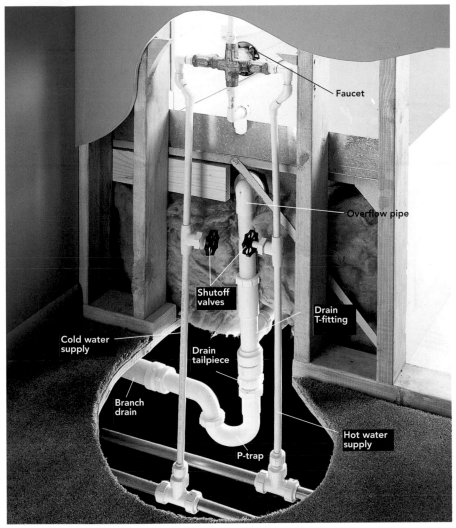

- Faucet
- Overflow pipe
- Shutoff valves
- Drain T-fitting
- Cold water supply
- Drain tailpiece
- Branch drain
- Hot water supply
- P-trap

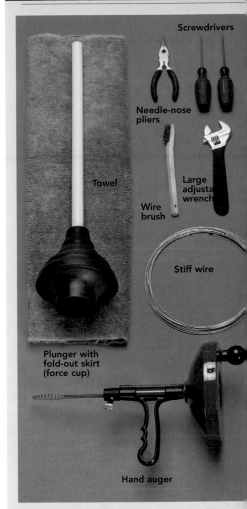

- Screwdrivers
- Needle-nose pliers
- Towel
- Large adjustable wrench
- Wire brush
- Stiff wire
- Plunger with fold-out skirt (force cup)
- Hand auger

If you removed the wall behind your tub/shower along with part of the floor, this is pretty much what you would see. From the photo you can tell that having to access your drain for outside the tub is not easy, and that maintaining the drain system to avoid major problems and blockages is well worth the effort. Fortunately, maintenance is not difficult, and minor clogs are relatively easy to track down and eliminate.

SKILLS YOU'LL NEED

- Vigorous plunging
- Using an auger

TERMS YOU NEED TO KNOW

POP-UP DRAIN—a mechanical drain stopper where a metal drain cover is raised and lowered with a lever mounted on the cover of the overflow opening.

PLUNGER-TYPE DRAIN—another mechanical drain stopper where a plunger is lowered through the overflow pipe to block the drain.

HAND AUGER—a long bendable cable with a crank at one end that is snaked into a drain line to retrieve or break up a blockage.

DIFFICULTY LEVEL

SKILLS LEVEL

EASY   MODERATE

Time: ½ to 1½ hours

HOW TO FIX A PLUNGER-TYPE DRAIN

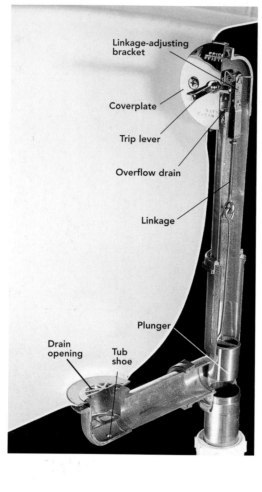

Linkage-adjusting bracket

Coverplate

Trip lever

Overflow drain

Linkage

Plunger

Drain opening

Tub shoe

1 A plunger-type tub drain has a simple grate over the drain opening and a behind-the-scenes plunger stopper. Remove the screws on the overflow coverplate with a slotted or Phillips head screwdriver. Pull the coverplate, linkage, and plunger from the overflow opening.

3 Adjust the plunger. If your tub isn't holding water with the plunger down, it's possible the plunger is hanging too high to fully block water from the tub shoe. Loosen the locknut with needlenose pliers then screw the rod down about ⅛". Tighten the locknut down. If your tub drains poorly, the plunger may be set too low. Loosen the locknut and screw the rod in an ⅛" before retightening the locknut.

2 Clean hair and soap off the plunger with a scrub brush. Mineral buildup is best tackled with white vinegar and a toothbrush or a small wire brush.

HOW TO FIX A POP-UP DRAIN

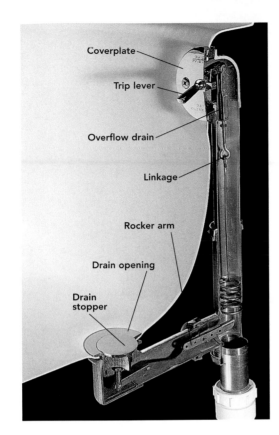

Coverplate
Trip lever
Overflow drain
Linkage
Rocker arm
Drain opening
Drain stopper

1 Raise the trip lever to the open position. Pull the stopper and rocker arm assembly from the drain. Clean off soap and hair with a dishwashing brush in a basin of hot water. Clean off mineral deposits with a toothbrush or small wire brush and white vinegar.

2 Remove the screws from the cover plate. Pull the trip lever and the linkage from the overflow opening. Clean off soap and hair with a dish scrubbing brush in a basin of hot water. Remove mineral buildup with white vinegar and a wire brush. Lubricate moving parts of the linkage and rocker arm mechanism with heatproof grease.

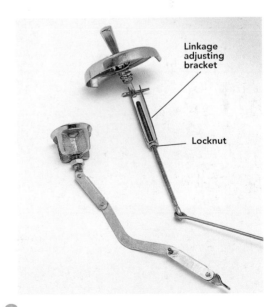

Linkage adjusting bracket
Locknut

3 Adjust the pop-up stopper mechanism by first loosening the locknut on the lift rod. If the stopper doesn't close all the way, shorten the linkage by screwing the rod ⅛" farther into the linkage-adjusting bracket. If the stopper doesn't open wide enough, extend the linkage by unscrewing the rod ⅛". Tighten the locknut before replacing the mechanism and testing your adjustment.

HOW TO CLEAR A SHOWER OR TUB DRAIN

1 To plunge a shower drain, first remove the drain stopper equipment, including the strainer cover (if there is one) from the drain of a tub or shower. Pop the strainer out with a screwdriver, or remove a screw in the middle. Clear any hair from the pipe below the drain with a stiff bent wire.

TIP: If you can't clear a stubborn clog with a plunger, insert the tip of a hand auger into the drain opening (see next page and pages 42 to 43).

2 If you can't see and remove an obstruction in the drain, try plunging. Position the plunger over the drain opening. If using a force-cup type of plunger, as seen above, fold the skirt up inside the plunger head. Completely cover the plunger with water. Plunge rhythmically through half-a-dozen ups and downs with increasing vigor, then yank up hard on the plunger. Repeat this cycle for up to 15 minutes. Promising signs: crud from the clog may rise into the tub before the weight of the water pushes the clog down the drain.

MAINTENANCE TIP

Like bathroom sinks, tubs and showers face an ongoing onslaught from soap and hair. When paired, this pesky combination is a sure-fire source of clogs. The soap scum coagulates as it is washed down the drain and binds the hair together in a mass that grows larger with every shower or bath. To nip these clogs in the bud, simply pour boiling hot clean water down the drain from time to time to melt the soapy mass and wash the binder away.

USING A HAND AUGER ON A SHOWER DRAIN

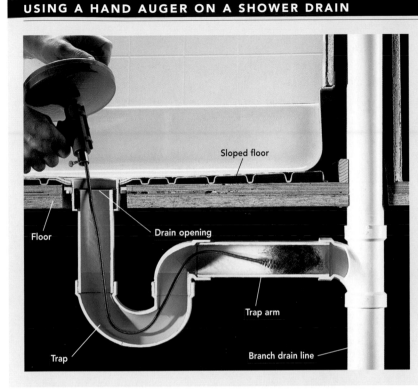

Floor

Sloped floor

Drain opening

Trap

Trap arm

Branch drain line

On shower drains, feed the head of the auger in through the *drain opening* after removing the strainer. Crank the handle of the auger to extend the cable and the auger head down into the trap and, if the clog is further downline, toward the branch drain. When clearing any drain, it is always better to retrieve the clog than to push it further downline. See pages 42 to 43.

USING A HAND AUGER ON A TUB DRAIN

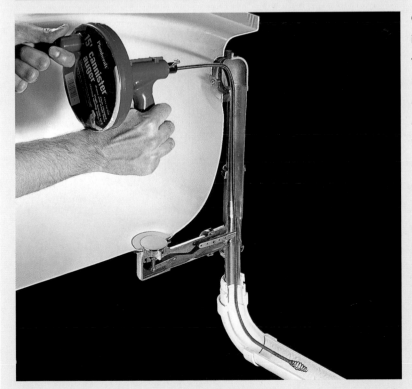

On combination tub/showers, it's generally easiest to insert the auger through the *overflow opening* after removing the coverplate and lifting out the drain linkage (see pages 70 to 71 for more information on drain linkages). Crank the handle of the auger to extend the cable and the auger head down into the trap and, if the clog is further downline, toward the branch drain. When clearing any drain, it is always better to retrieve the clog than to push it further downline. See pages 42 to 43 for more information on using an auger.

Kitchen Sink Stopped (and Disposer Too?)

11

Drain clearing isn't all drudgery and filth. Some people find the plunger to be as much a tool of personal transformation as an implement for removing clogs.

IT'S A WEEK TO PAYDAY, and that austerity plan you've arranged with your creditors gives you 67 dollars and change to last until then. Alas, the kitchen sink is clogged; you can't afford a plumber! Don't despair—your enemy is merely a wad of coffee grounds and some bacon fat. If plunging doesn't work, you'll go after it where it lives, remove the trap, look in the disposer, explore the fixture drain with a hand auger. With the right tool, you are like Thor and his thunderbolt, Zeus and his trident. You, we are confident, will locate the clog and break it up or drag it into the light, slap it into a basin, and sluice its slimy spawn into the sewer with a triumphant blast of tap water. You. Will. Win.

TIP: Avoid chemical clog removers. They can damage your pipes, your fixtures, and you, and they don't work very well. They're so dangerous to people, in fact, that drain cleaning services often charge extra if you've used them prior to their visit.

KITCHEN SINKS 101

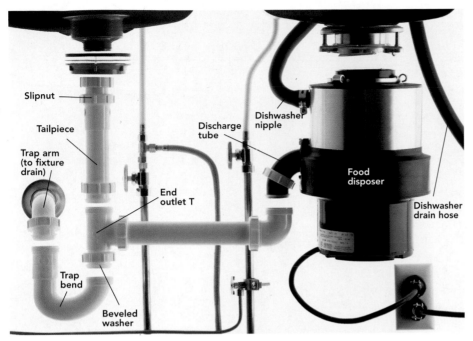

- Slipnut
- Tailpiece
- Trap arm (to fixture drain)
- Discharge tube
- Dishwasher nipple
- End outlet T
- Food disposer
- Dishwasher drain hose
- Trap bend
- Beveled washer

Kitchen sink drain components are usually connected with *slipnuts*, which means everything from the *tailpiece* beneath a basket strainer to the *trap arm* can be removed for cleaning. Clogs commonly occur in the *trap bend* and the *end outlet T*. With the trap arm off, the *fixture drain* can be augered. Make sure your *beveled washers* are facing the right direction when you put things back together. Clogs can happen in the *discharge tube* and *drain chamber* of a disposer. The *impellers* in the grinding chamber of a disposer can get stuck to the *grinding ring* with tough or fibrous waste materials. The *dishwasher drain hose* should be clamped where it joins the disposer if you wish to plunge the sink drain.

TERMS YOU NEED TO KNOW

BASKET STRAINER—This is the typical strainer, plug, and drain found on a kitchen sink that doesn't have a disposer.

TAILPIECE—takes the waste from the basket strainer to the trap.

GRINDING CHAMBER—the chamber visible through the drain of a disposer where wastes are ground.

IMPELLER—one of two or four steel lugs on the metal plate at the bottom of a disposer grinding chamber. Its function is to push food waste against the grinding ring as the plate rotates.

GRINDING RING—a stationary, toothed ring at the bottom perimeter of the disposer grinding chamber. Food wastes are ground against it until they are small enough to be washed into the drain chamber below.

TOOLS & SUPPLIES YOU'LL NEED

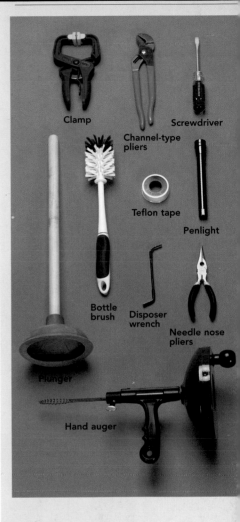

- Clamp
- Channel-type pliers
- Screwdriver
- Teflon tape
- Penlight
- Bottle brush
- Disposer wrench
- Needle nose pliers
- Plunger
- Hand auger

SKILLS YOU'LL NEED

- Working with slip joints
- Plunging
- Flexibility

DIFFICULTY LEVEL

SKILLS LEVEL

EASY   HARD

Time: ½ to 1½ hours.

KITCHEN SINK STOPPED? PLUNGE IN

CLEARING THE TRAP AND BEYOND

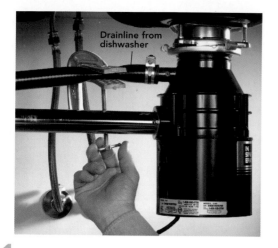

1 Plunging a kitchen sink is not difficult, but you need to create an uninterrupted pressure lock between the plunger and the clog. If you have a dishwasher, the drain tube needs to be clamped shut and sealed off at the disposer or drainline. The pads on the clamp should be large enough to flatten the tube across its full diameter (or you can clamp the tube ends between small boards).

2 If there is a second basin, have a helper hold a basket strainer plug in its drain or put a large pot or bucket full of water on top of it. If you just set the strainer plug in place, the pressure of your plunging will pop the plug instead of the clog. Unfold the skirt within the plunger and place this in the drain of the sink you are plunging. There should be enough water in the sink to cover the plunger head. Plunge rhythmically for six repetitions with increasing vigor, pulling up hard on the last rep. Repeat this sequence until the clog or you are vanquished. Flush out a cleared clog with plenty of hot water.

1 If plunging doesn't work, remove the trap and clean it out. With the trap off, see if water flows freely from both sinks (if you have two). Sometimes clogs will lodge in the T-fitting or one of the waste pipes feeding it. These may be pulled out manually or cleared with a bottlebrush or wire. When reassembling the trap, apply Teflon tape clockwise to the male threads of metal waste pieces. Tighten with your channel-type pliers. Plastic pieces need no tape and should be hand-tightened only.

2 If you suspect the clog is downstream of the trap, remove the trap arm from the fitting at the wall. Look in the fixture drain with a penlight. If you see water, that means the fixture drain is plugged. Clear it with a hand auger (p. 73).

DISPOSER NOT GRINDING?

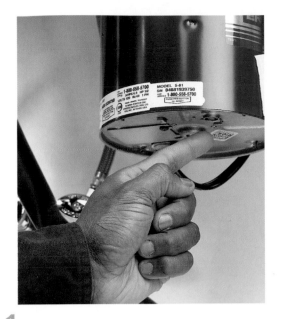

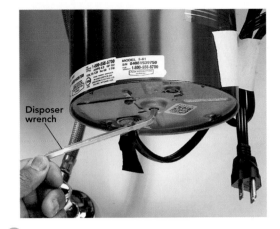

1 Press the reset button located on the base of the disposer and switch the appliance on. If the motor hums but cannot move, the grinders are clogged and need to be cleared.

2 Unplug the disposer. Look for a wrench with a hex shaped head that came with the disposer. Stick this in a fitting in the base of the disposer. This manipulates the metal plate that holds the impellers. Typically, some hard or fibrous object is binding an impeller to the grinding ring. Rock the plate back and forth with the wrench to unbind the impeller. You can also attempt to rotate the plate from above by pushing against an impeller with a broom handle.

Unplug disposer before inserting tools

DRAINING SLOWLY?

3 Look for and remove any material that's keeping the metal plate from rotating. Make sure the disposer is unplugged and then shine a light into the disposer and look for hard or fibrous debris between the impellers and the grinding ring. Use needlenose pliers to pull debris free.

Waste buildup in the drain chamber beneath the impeller disc can lead to a slow-draining disposer. Remove the discharge elbow from the disposer body by withdrawing one or two screws or bolts. These may require a screwdriver or an adjustable wrench. Clear debris from the discharge elbow then shine a light into the drain chamber. Reach into the drain chamber with needlenose pliers to remove any fibrous buildup.

12

Leaky Sink Strainer

If your waste water takes a wrong turn on the way to the sewer, it may be time to reseat, or replace, your sink strainer.

THE SINK STRAINER IS THE PERFORATED BASKET IN THE BOTTOM OF YOUR KITCHEN SINK THAT CATCHES SPAGHETTI AND BROCCOLI SPEARS BEFORE THEY DIVE DOWN THE DRAIN. If your sink is simply not holding water, you may need to replace only the basket. These are available at any hardware store. If water is leaking onto the floor in the cabinet, you may need to reseat or replace the sink strainer body. A replacement includes the basket and the metal well that cradles the basket and forms a seal with your sink and the drain pipe.

FIXING A LEAKY SINK STRAINER

1 Clear out the cabinet under the sink. Unscrew slipnuts from both ends of the drain tailpiece with channel-type pliers. Lower the tailpiece into the trap bend or remove the tailpiece. NOTE: If you have a double sink and your tailpiece is very short, you may need to loosen slipnuts elsewhere and remove a larger piece of the drain assembly to access the strainer body.

2 Loosen the locknut with a spud wrench or channel-type pliers. Unthread the locknut completely, then push the strainer body up out of the sink.

3 Remove old putty from the drain opening with a putty knife. If reusing the old strainer body, clean off the old putty from under the flange. Knead plumber's putty into a warm, soft snake and apply to the lip of the drain opening. Press the strainer body into the drain opening. Any writing on the strainer should be read from the front.

4 From under the sink, place the rubber gasket and the friction washer over the strainer body and secure the body to the sink deck with the locknut. Tap the nubs on the locknut with a screwdriver to tighten it. Reattach the drain by tightening the slipnut over the threaded end of the tailpiece.

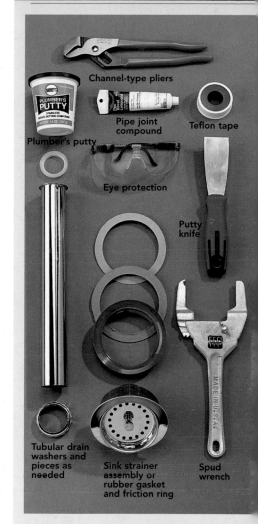
NSKILLS YOU'LL NEED

- Using wrenches
- Putty rolling
- Making slip-joint connections

DIFFICULTY LEVEL

SKILLS LEVEL

EASY   MODERATE

Time: ½ to 1 hour plus shopping

TERMS YOU NEED TO KNOW

PLUMBER'S PUTTY—a clay-like material used to seal metal hardware to the sink.

TEFLON TAPE—a thin white tape used to lubricate and seal threaded fittings and keep them from sticking together.

PIPE JOINT COMPOUND—a paste that may be used instead of Teflon tape.

BASKET STRAINER—another name for a sink strainer.

13

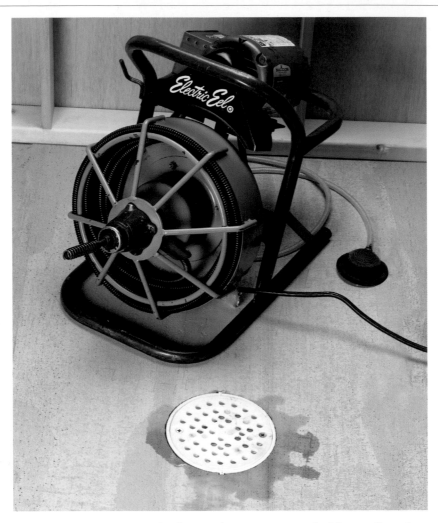

When the going gets tough, the tough rent power tools. The medium duty auger shown here is perfect for augering the 2-inch-diameter floor drainlines and branch drainlines.

WHEN PLUNGERS AND HAND AUGERS MEET A CLOG THEY CAN'T DISLODGE, you have one more DIY option before you call a professional drain cleaning service. Most rental centers stock power augers in several sizes. These electric tools work in much the same manner as a hand auger, but with much more tenacity. With spear tools, cutting tools, and spring tools, they can push or cut through a clog, or snag an object and drag it out from your floor or branch drainline.

Always read the instructions carefully and be sure to get through operating instructions at the rental center. If used improperly, power augers can cause major damage to your plumbing system. They are designed to be inserted beyond the trap or through cleanouts in the drainline, so they do not need to be forced through the drain trap. Never run a power auger through a toilet—it could scratch the porcelain or even break the fixture.

POWER AUGERING 101

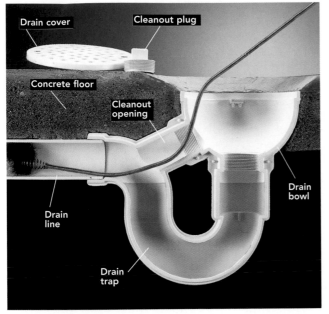

Drain cover
Cleanout plug
Concrete floor
Cleanout opening
Drain bowl
Drain line
Drain trap

Floor drains can develop extremely robust clogs, especially if the drain cover is absent. A *power auger* that's inserted through the cleanout opening can travel 50 feet or more to hunt down and remove stubborn clogs. These rental tools come in several sizes and may also be used to clear tub/shower drainlines, branch drainlines and even a 3- to 4-inch diameter soil stack or house drain.

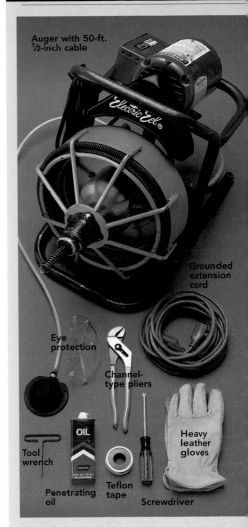
TOOL TIP

Power augers can be fitted with three different head styles. The spring tool is affixed to the cable end to snag and retrieve an obstruction. The spear tool is used to penetrate a clog and puncture it to create a starter hole for the cutting tool, which can cut apart very resistant clogs (often tree roots).

Spring tool

Spear tool

Cutter tool

SKILLS YOU'LL NEED

- Driving to rental center
- Exercising caution

DIFFICULTY LEVEL

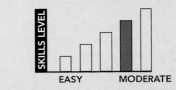

SKILLS LEVEL

EASY   MODERATE

Time: ½ to 1 hour plus renting equipment

TERMS YOU NEED TO KNOW

TRAP—a U-shaped bend of drain pipe behind or under every fixture. It's always full of water to keep sewer gases from rising into the house. If possible, remove the trap before augering the drainline to a fixture. With the floor drain, you bypass the trap by opening a cleanout plug.

CLEANOUTS—are access ports in drain pipes kept covered with threaded caps.

CLEANING TOOL—the spring, spear, or cutter attached to the tip of a cable auger. These are interchangeable.

BRANCH OR FIXTURE DRAIN—the run of pipe in the wall or floor that drains a fixture (except a toilet). It's usually 1½ to 2-inches in diameter. It may join with a toilet drain, a stack, or the house drain.

HOW TO POWER-AUGER A FLOOR DRAIN

If you choose to auger a larger line, you may find yourself opening a cleanout with 10 or 20 vertical feet of waste water behind it. Be careful. The cap may unexpectedly burst open when it's loose enough, spewing noxious waste water uncontrollably over anything in its path, including you! Here are some precautions:

Whenever possible, remove a trap or cleanout close to the top of the backed-up water level. Run your auger through this. Make sure the auger and its electric connections will not get wet should waste water spew forcefully from the cleanout opening.

Use the spear tool on the power auger first, to let the water drain out through a smaller hole before widening it with a larger cutting tool. If you are augering through a 3- or 4-inch cleanout, use three bits: the spear, a small cutter, and then a larger cutter to do the best job.

1 Remove the cover from the floor drain using a slotted or Phillips screwdriver. On one wall of the drain bowl you'll see a cleanout plug. Remove the cleanout plug from the drain bowl with your largest channel-type pliers. This cleanout allows you to bypass the trap. If it's stuck, apply penetrating oil to the threads and let it sit a half an hour before trying to free it again. If the wrench won't free it, rent a large pipe wrench from your home center or hardware store. You can also auger through the trap if you have to.

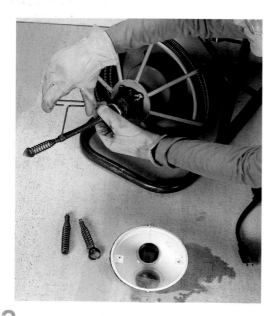

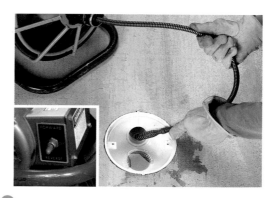

3 Wear close-fitting clothing and contain long hair. Place the power auger machine in a dry location within three feet of the drain opening. Plug the tool into a grounded, Ground Fault Interrupted (GFI) protected circuit. Put on eye protection and gloves; you will be holding a rotating metal cable and may be exposed to dangerous bacteria and caustic drain cleaning chemicals. Position the footswitch where it is easy to actuate; visualize using the machine without having to overreach the rotating drum or exposed belts. Make sure the FOR/REV switch is in the Forward position (inset photo). Hand feed the cleaning tool and some cable into the drain or cleanout before turning the machine on.

2 Rent an electric drum auger with at least 50 feet of ½-inch cable. The rental company should provide a properly sized, grounded extension cord, heavy leather gloves, and eye protection. The auger should come with a spear tool, cutter tool, and possibly a spring-tool suitable for a 2-inch drainline. Attach the spearhead first (with the machine unplugged).

4 Stationary power augers (as opposed to pistol-grip types) are controlled by a foot pedal called an actuator so you can turn the power on and off hands-free.

6 Gradually work through the clog by pulling back on the cable whenever the machine starts to bog down and pushing it forward again when it gains new momentum. Again, never let the cable stop turning when the motor is running. When you have broken through the clog (or if you are using the spring head and believe you have snagged an object) withdraw the cable from the line. Manually pull the cable from the drain line while continuing to run the drum Forward. If it's practical, have a helper hose off the cable as its withdrawn and recoiled. When the cleaning tool is close to the drain opening, release the foot actuator and let the cable come to a stop before feeding the remaining two or three feet of cable into the drum by hand.

5 With both gloved hands on the cable, depress the foot actuator to start the machine. Gradually push the rotating cable into the drain opening. If the rotation slows or you cannot feed more cable into the drain, pull back on the cable before pushing it forward again. Don't force it. The cable needs to be rotating whenever the motor is running or it can kink and buckle, destroying the cable (although a clutch on the drum should prevent this). If the cleaning tool becomes stuck, turn the FOR/REV switch to Reverse and back the tool off the obstruction before switching back to Forward again.

7 After clearing the drain pipe, run the auger through the trap. Finish cleaning the auger. Wrap Teflon tape clockwise onto the plug threads and replace the plug. Run hot water through a hose from the laundry sink or use a bucket to flush remaining debris through the trap and down the line.

Repairing Outside Faucets

14

A leaky outside faucet on a house (called a sillcock or a hose bib) usually is easier to repair than to replace. Because they must withstand cold temperatures, you won't find plastic cartridges in outdoor faucet bodies. Repairs are made in much the same way as for interior compression faucets (see pages 30 to 31).

COMMON AILMENTS OF OUTSIDE FAUCETS include broken or loose handles, dripping spouts, and dripping handles. In the north, outside faucets and their pipes can crack when the water inside them freezes. Outside faucets with hoses or sprinkler systems attached pose another hazard: if water pressure is lost in the house or the community, water may flow backwards in the pipes, drawing potentially polluted water through the hose and into the house or even into the municipal system. For this reason, local plumbing codes often require that a vacuum breaker be attached to faucets that are threaded for hoses. In this section we'll show you how to identify and fix the most common leak causes.

OUTSIDE FAUCETS 101

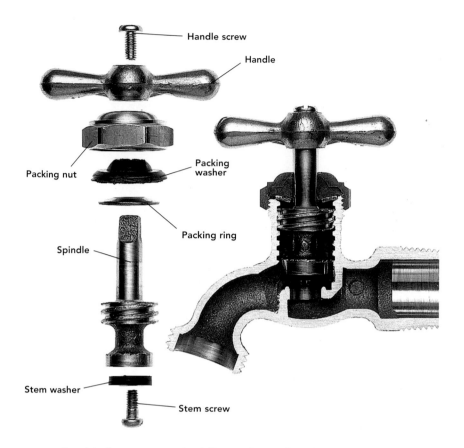

- Handle screw
- Handle
- Packing nut
- Packing washer
- Packing ring
- Spindle
- Stem washer
- Stem screw

Outside faucets come in different forms, but their valves, which are the mechanism that turns off the water, are always compression style. Ordinary outdoor faucets, like the *hose bib* above, need to be shut off and drained before winter in cold climates. This is done inside the house at a stop and waste valve.

HOSE BIB—a faucet with male threads on the spout to accept female hose threads.

SILLCOCK—a hose bib with a wide flange at the base allowing it to be attached to an exterior wall with screws.

COMPRESSION VALVE—a valve type with the components shown above.

STEM WASHER—When the faucet is off, it is pressed over the intake hole in the faucet by the spindle. Drips at the spout usually involve a worn stem washer.

VALVE SEAT—This forms the rim of the hole plugged by the stem washer. A damaged seat will wear out the stem washer.

PACKING—the neoprene washer or other material pressed below the packing nut that prevents water from leaking out below the handle when the faucet is on.

TOOLS & SUPPLIES YOU'LL NEED

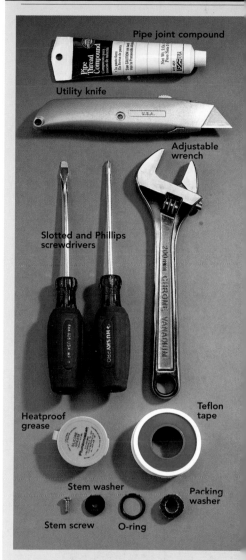

- Pipe joint compound
- Utility knife
- Adjustable wrench
- Slotted and Phillips screwdrivers
- Teflon tape
- Heatproof grease
- Stem washer
- Packing washer
- Stem screw
- O-ring

SKILLS YOU'LL NEED

- Using an adjustable wrench
- Using a screwdriver

DIFFICULTY LEVEL

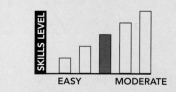

SKILLS LEVEL

EASY   MODERATE

Time: less than an hour plus shopping

HOW TO REPAIR A LEAKY OUTSIDE FAUCET

1 Turn off the water to your outside faucet and open the faucet to drain any remaining water (this step may be skipped if you are only replacing the handle). The shutoff valve is usually located on the water supply line, close to the faucet on the interior side of the wall. Outdoor faucets have only one supply pipe (cold).

2 Remove the handle from an outside faucet by removing the handle screw and pulling the handle straight off. If the handle is damaged, bring it to the hardware store and find a replacement with the same size spindle hole. Screw the new handle on if the faucet does not leak.

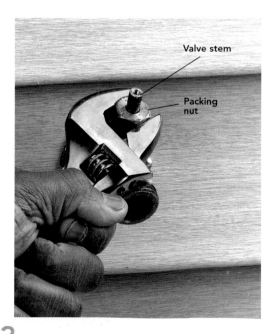

Valve stem

Packing nut

3 Unscrew the packing nut that secures the spindle to the valve body, using an adjustable wrench. If the nut resists, hold the faucet body with a pipe wrench to stabilize it while you bear down on the nut.

Packing washer

4 Pry off the packing washer and packing ring from the top of the spindle and inspect their general condition. If they are worn or damaged, bring them to the hardware store to purchase a replacement. NOTE: Instead of a washer, some older compression faucets (including hose bibs) have a wad of packing string stuffed into the packing nut to seal the spindle (see page 89).

Stem sleeve

5 Pull out the spindle. With some faucets, a stem sleeve holding the spindle will also need to be unscrewed to remove the spindle. Be careful not to damage the male threads of the packing nut when removing this sleeve.

7 Secure the stem washer to the spindle using the stem screw. Coat the new stem washer with heatproof grease and coat the threads of the stem screw with pipe joint compound.

6 Remove the stem screw on the other end of the spindle with a screwdriver and remove and inspect the stem washer (the stem washer is the most likely suspect if the faucet is dripping). Bring the screw and spindle along with the washer to a hardware store or home center to get a matching washer and, if needed, a new screw that fits your spindle. A replacement washer needs to fit within the brass cup on the spindle and have the same profile (typically flat) as the old washer.

SAFETY TIP

An anti-siphon device is required for outdoor faucets and indoor hose bibs. The requirement doesn't apply to old faucets being repaired, but it's still a good idea to use one. The most popular retrofit anti-siphon devices are simply twisted onto the nozzle of the hose bib.

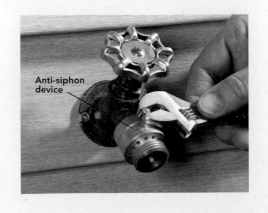

Anti-siphon device

REPAIRING A LEAKY OUTSIDE FAUCET (CONTINUED)

WHAT IF...?

What if I have a freezeless faucet?

Take apart and replace washers and O-rings on a freezeless faucet as you would a regular outside faucet, but with some differences noted as follows:

Stabilize the valve body of the faucet with channel-type pliers before twisting off the packing nut with an adjustable wrench. This will help you avoid torquing the long body of the faucet.

You may need to put the handle back on the spindle after removing the packing nut in order to rotate the spindle into an orientation that will allow it to be pulled out of the valve body.

The stem washer is on the end of a very long spindle with this type of faucet. This allows the water to be shut off in the above-freezing part of the house. Take the spindle to a hardware or plumbing store to get the right replacement washers and O-ring.

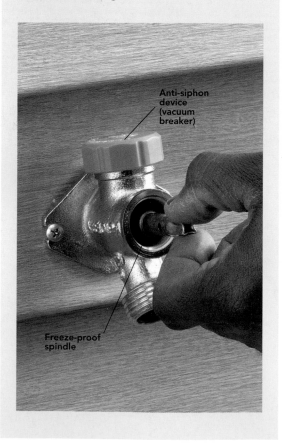

Anti-siphon device (vacuum breaker)

Freeze-proof spindle

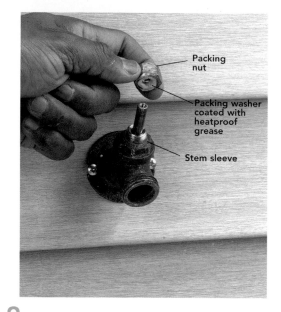

Packing nut

Packing washer coated with heatproof grease

Stem sleeve

8   Install the valve stem, replacing the stem sleeve. Coat the new packing washer with heat-proof grease and slip it and the packing ring, if present, onto the free spindle end (or install it in the packing nut). Apply pipe joint compound to the valve body threads and refasten the packing nut. **NOTE:** Instead of packing, some faucets use an O-ring on the spindle to keep water in the valve. Remove and replace it.

9   Slip the new faucet handle onto the spindle end and secure it with the handle screw.

VARIATION: USING PACKING STRING

1 Wrap two or three layers of Teflon tape clockwise around the male threads on the valve body before tightening on the packing nut with your adjustable wrench. Complete the repair as in the previous sequence. If the faucet drips from the handle, remove it and add more packing string (along with fresh Teflon tape).

2 If your old faucet is sealed with packing string and not a packing washer or an O-ring (or if you can't find a packing washer that fits), remake the seal between the valve stem and the packing nut with new packing string. Packing string is impregnated with graphite. Wrap the new packing string onto the valve stem above the stem sleeve so it's about 1½ times as thick as the thickness of the gap between the stem and the packing nut. You may need to adjust the amount of string you use to create a seal but still leave enough room to tighten on the packing nut.

WINTERIZING YOUR HOSE BIB

Even if you have a freezeless faucet, you need to take the hoses off your outdoor faucets, since these can hold water in the faucet, which can freeze and crack the valve or pipe. Unless you have a freezeless faucet, you also need to turn off your outside faucet from the inside and drain the faucet before below-freezing temperatures settle in. Find the shutoff valve on the branch pipe leading to your outside faucet and close it. Check to see if the valve has a waste valve on the side. If so, use it to drain the water in the line between the valve and the hose bib after opening the outside hose bib. You can also add a cover to the hose bib (see page 95).

WARNING: If you have a sprinkler system, its lines should be professionally cleared for the winter with pressurized air.

Waste valve

15

Adding a Shower to a Tub

Converting a plain bathtub into a tub/shower is a relatively easy task when you use a flexible shower adapter that fits onto a special replacement tub spout.

FORGET THE LAZY 8 TRUCK STOP. Forget the locker room at the health club. You may be able to enjoy the luxury of a real shower right in your own home or apartment. If you have an old built-in tub but no shower, we'll show you how you can remove the spout and replace it with one equipped with an adapter hose outlet. A flexible shower hose can be screwed to this. We'll also show you how to install a mounting bracket so you can hang the showerhead and free up your hands. Add a telescoping shower curtain rod and a shower curtain and your new shower stall is ready for duty.

SHOWER ADAPTERS 101

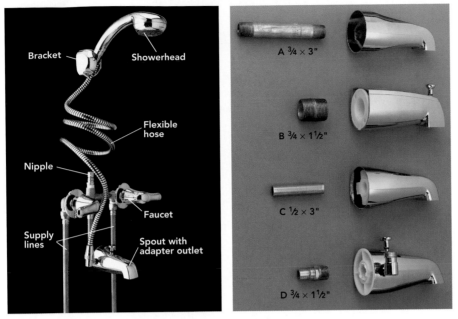

Bracket

Showerhead

Flexible hose

Nipple

Faucet

Supply lines

Spout with adapter outlet

A ¾ × 3"

B ¾ × 1½"

C ½ × 3"

D ¾ × 1½"

The appearance of the spout gives good clues as to which kind of nipple it is connected to. A) Spout with no diverter is probably connected to a 3" long threaded nipple. To install a diverter spout you'll need to replace the 3" threaded nipple with a shorter threaded nipple that sticks out no more than ½" from the wall—not too big of a job. B) If the spout already has a diverter knob, it already has a showerhead, and you're doing the wrong project (although there is no reason you couldn't hook up a shower adapter if you want a handheld shower). C) If the spout has a small setscrew in a slot on the underside, it is probably attached with a slip fitting to a ½" copper supply nipple. Unless you are able to solder a new transition fitting onto the old pipe after cutting it, call a plumber to install the new spout here. D) Spouts with outlets for shower adapters require a short threaded nipple (or comparable union) that sticks out from the wall no more than ¾".

NTERMS YOU NEED TO KNOW

NIPPLE—a short piece of iron or brass pipe that's threaded on both ends. It may be unscrewed from the wall.

COPPER STUB—a short piece of copper pipe with or without a threaded adapter on the end. It cannot be unscrewed from the wall.

REDUCING BUSHING—a little piece of pipe with interior and exterior threads. In this case, to allow a ¾-inch tub spout to screw onto a ½-inch nipple.

TEFLON TAPE—a white or thin tape wound on pipe threads to seal and lubricate the joint.

TOOLS & SUPPLIES YOU'LL NEED

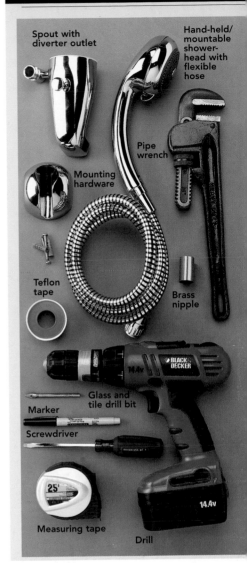

Spout with diverter outlet

Hand-held/ mountable showerhead with flexible hose

Pipe wrench

Mounting hardware

Teflon tape

Brass nipple

Glass and tile drill bit

Marker

Screwdriver

25'

14.4v

14.4v

Measuring tape

Drill

SKILLS YOU'LL NEED

- Making pipe connections
- Cutting tile or tileboard
- Working with wall anchors

DIFFICULTY LEVEL

SKILLS LEVEL

EASY   MODERATE

Time: 1 to 2 hours

HOW TO ADD A SHOWER WITH AN ADAPTER SPOUT

1 Make sure the old spout is not held in place with a setscrew (see previous page) and then remove it by wrapping it with a cloth and turning the spout with channel-type pliers or a pipe wrench.

TOOL TIP

A long-bladed screwdriver or a dowel inserted into the mouth of the spout can be used to spin the spout free from the nipple.

2 If you have a long iron or brass nipple like this, you need to replace it with a short one. Threaded nipples have threads at each end, so you can usually unscrew the old ones. Mark the nipple at the face of the wall and write "front" on your side. Unscrew it counterclockwise with a pipe wrench. Get a threaded brass nipple of the same diameter that is about half an inch longer than the distance from the back of your old nipple to your line.

3 Wrap six layers of Teflon tape clockwise on the nipple and thread into the wall. Thread the reducing bushing onto the nipple if it will fit. Thread the adapter spout on. Tighten further with a screwdriver or dowel to orient the spout correctly.

4 Attach flexible shower hose to the adapter hose outlet. Tighten with an adjustable wrench.

5 Determine the location of showerhead bracket. Use hose length as a guide, and make sure showerhead can be easily lifted off the bracket.

6 Mark hole locations. Obtain a glass-and-tile drill bit for your electric drill in the size recommended by the shower bracket manufacturer. Put on eye protection and drill holes in ceramic tile on your marks.

7 Insert anchors into holes, and tap in place with a wooden or rubber mallet. Fasten showerhead holder to the wall using a Phillips screwdriver and the mounting screws.

Preventing Frozen Pipes

16

Spending a little time and money on protecting your water pipes from freezing is one of the best investments a homeowner can make.

BURST FREEZING PIPES lead to about a quarter million families suffering catastrophic water damage to their houses each year. That's the big picture. The small picture works like this: A section of one of your hot or cold water pipes is exposed to below freezing temperatures. You don't use the water in that pipe during the time it takes for an ice plug to develop. As the ice plug grows, it compresses the water between the plug and the faucet(s) at the end of that line. The pressure becomes extreme and bursts the pipe, sometimes in an area away from the ice plug. The plug thaws. Water spews out of the crack, irreparably damaging walls, floors and your possessions. Another scenario goes like this: You take immediate action to thaw and relieve pressure on frozen pipes and then take short- and long-term steps to prevent refreezing. We'll give you pointers here.

FREEZE-PROOFING 101

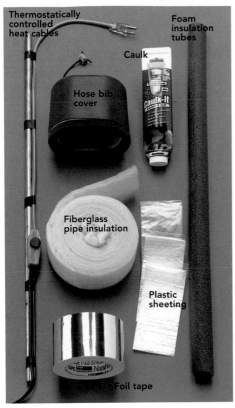

Thermostatically controlled heat cables
Foam insulation tubes
Caulk
Hose bib cover
Fiberglass pipe insulation
Plastic sheeting
Foil tape

Paintable acrylic caulk is good for sealing small gaps, especially in areas where appearance is important. Pipe insulation products include narrow strips of *fiberglass*, *foam insulation tubes* sized to fit common pipe sizes, and *preformed valve covers* for protecting outdoor faucets (hose bibs). *Foil tape* may be used to secure and seal pipe insulation products. *Thermostatically controlled heat cables* prevent pipes that are exposed to long periods of below freezing temperatures from freezing. Expanding foam (not shown here) is effective for stopping large cold air leaks, although it can be unsightly.

HOW TO THAW PIPES:

Open the faucet affected by the frozen pipe. Beginning at the faucet, use a hair dryer to warm the pipe, working back toward the likely area of the freeze. Leave water on until full flow is restored, then take steps to prevent refreezing. If the pipe has burst, see pages 116 to 119. WARNING: Never use an open flame to thaw pipes.

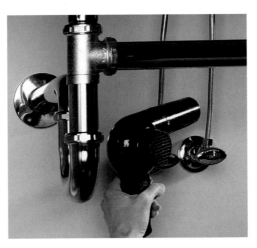

TERMS YOU NEED TO KNOW

CPVC—This is a kind of plastic water pipe that's incompatible with some kinds of foam insulation (which cause it to soften) and needs to be protected with foil if heat tape is used.

THERMAL ENVELOPE—is the sometimes-murky boundary that divides heated from unheated space. Inside spaces that may be outside the thermal envelope include crawl spaces, attics, garages, basements, and three-season rooms. Pipes that may need your attention are those near or outside the thermal envelope.

TOOLS & SUPPLIES YOU'LL NEED

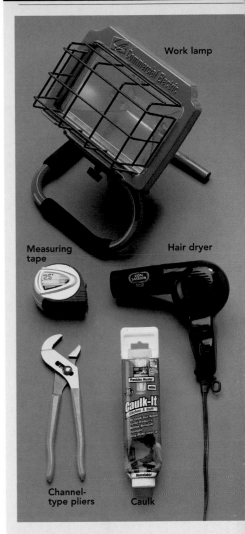

Work lamp
Measuring tape
Hair dryer
Channel-type pliers
Caulk

SKILLS YOU'LL NEED

- Investigative skills
- Cutting and fitting

DIFFICULTY LEVEL

SKILLS LEVEL

EASY   MODERATE

Time: variable

HOW TO FROST-PROOF YOUR PLUMBING

OUTDOOR FAUCETS. Remove hoses from all outside faucets when freezing weather approaches. Shut off the water to the faucet at the shutoff valve inside. Drain the pipe from the shut off to the spout by opening a waste nut on the shutoff and the outside faucet itself. (See "Replacing an Outside Faucet with a Frost Proof Sillcock," pages 138 to 139.)

PIPES NEAR EXTERIOR WALLS. Permit air to circulate from the heated interior of the house to plumbing near outside walls. This could mean opening the dishwasher door and service panel, sink cabinet doors, and plumbed rooms that aren't heated directly. WARNING: Inappropriate warming of pipes is a major cause of house fires.

IMMINENT DANGER OF FREEZING. Leave vulnerable lines open to a fast drip if you suspect any of your supply pipes may be in imminent danger of freezing. Even slowly moving water will not freeze. This may not be water and energy efficient (although if you're around, you can collect water in a bucket), but it gives you time to come up with a permanent solution.

AIR LEAKS NEAR PIPES. Seal gaps that can jet cold air onto pipes. Use caulk for small gaps and expanding foam or fiberglass for large gaps. WARNING: Expanding foam expands more than you think it will and cures to an unsightly rust color when exposed to sun.

INSULATE SUPPLY PIPES. Insulate pipes that pass through unavoidably cold spaces like crawl spaces and attics. Measure a pipe's diameter by closing an adjustable wrench on it and then measuring the span of the wrench jaws. Measure the length of pipes to be insulated so you know how many linear feet of insulation to buy. Buy self-sealing side-slit foam tubes for pipes of your diameter(s). Cut double 45-degree notches with a scissors to turn corners (inset photo). Seal all slits and joints that are not self-adhering with foil tape.

PIPE UNIONS. For irregular and jointed pipes, use fiberglass strip insulation secured with foil tape. Wind the insulation in an overlapping spiral. The tape should not compress the fiberglass too tightly and should form a continuous vapor seal to prevent condensation on the pipes in the summer.

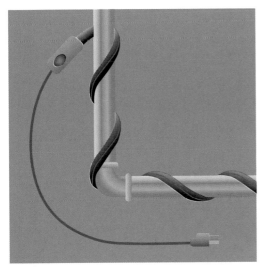

PIPES EXPOSED TO BELOW FREEZING TEMPERATURES for long periods will freeze, insulated or not. Wrap your most vulnerable pipes with U.L. approved thermostatically controlled heat cables according to manufacturer instructions. In the long run, these pipes should be moved to a more protected location or the thermal envelope should be extended to include the pipes.

WHILE YOU'RE AWAY. Don't set the thermostat below 55 degrees F, and have somebody who knows how to shut off the water check on the house daily.

Replacing a Bathtub Spout

17

The bathtub spout may need replacing for many reasons, including a failed diverter like the one above. You also may want to add a flexible shower adapter (see pages 90 to 93), or the old spout could just be disgusting beyond repair.

IN MANY SITUATIONS, REPLACING A BATHTUB SPOUT can be almost as easy as hooking up a garden hose to an outdoor spigot. There are some situations where it is a bit more difficult, but still pretty simple. The only time it's a real problem is when the spout is attached to a plain copper supply nipple, rather than a threaded nipple. You'll know this is the case if the spout has a setscrew on the underside where it meets the wall. Many bathtub spouts are sold in kits with a matching showerhead and handle or handles. But for a simple one-for-one replacement, spouts are sold separately. You just need to make sure the new spout is compatible with the existing nipple (see next page).

TUB SPOUTS 101

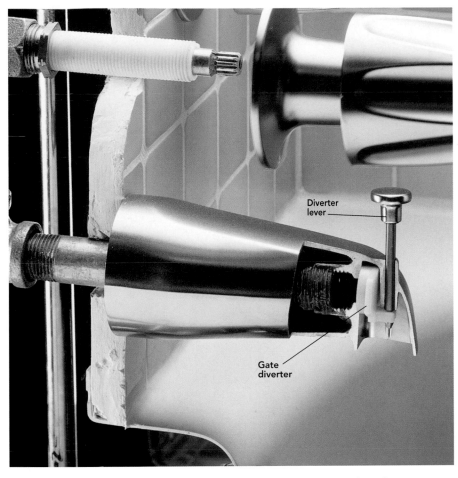

Diverter
lever

Gate
diverter

Masking
tape

Rags

Pliers

Adjustable pliers

Allen
wrenches

Screw-
drivers

Channel-type
pliers

Replacement spout

Utility
knife

Measuring
tape

Teflon tape

In many bathtub/shower plumbing systems, the *spout* has the important job of housing the diverter switch—a *gate* inside the spout that is operated by a lever with a knob for pulling. When the gate is open, water comes out of the spout when the faucet is turned on. When the *diverter* is pulled shut, the water is redirected up a *riser pipe* and to the *showerhead*. Failure of the diverter is one of the most common reasons for replacing a spout.

TERMS YOU NEED TO KNOW

TUB SPOUT GATE DIVERTER—a knob-operated gate valve on the tip of a tub spout. When it's pulled up, water cannot pass through the spout and is forced to rise to the showerhead.

HANDLE-OPERATED DIVERTER VALVE—the diverter valve behind the central handle on a three-handle faucet. It uses a compression stem and washer or a cartridge to divert water from the spout so the shower can be used.

SKILLS YOU'LL NEED

- Using channel-type pliers
- Tracking the order and arrangement of parts

DIFFICULTY LEVEL

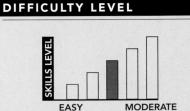

SKILLS LEVEL

EASY   MODERATE

Time: 1 hour plus research and shopping

HOW TO REPLACE A SLIP-FIT SPOUT

1 Slip fitting: Check underneath the tub spout to look for an access slot or cutout, which indicates the spout is a slip-fit style that is held in place with a setscrew and mounted on a copper supply nipple. Loosen the screw with a hex (Allen) wrench. Pull off the spout.

2 Clean the copper nipple with steel wool. If you find any sharp edges where the nipple was cut, smooth them out with emery paper. Then, insert the O-ring that comes with spout onto the nipple (see the manufacturer's instructions) and slide the spout body over the nipple in an upside-down position.

3 With the spout upside down for ease of access, tighten the setscrews on the clamp, working through the access slot or cutout, until you feel resistance.

4 Spin the spout so it's right-side up and then tighten the setscrew from below, making sure the wall end of the spout is flush against the wall. Do not overtighten the setscrew.

HOW TO REPLACE A THREADED SPOUT

1 If you see no setscrew or slot on the underside of the spout, it is attached to a threaded nipple. Unscrew the tub spout by inserting a heavy-duty flat screwdriver into the spout opening and spinning it counterclockwise.

TOOL TIP

Alternatively, grip the spout with a padded pipe wrench or channel-type pliers. Buy a compatible replacement spout at a home center or hardware store.

Copper nipple with threaded adapter

2 Wrap several courses of Teflon tape clockwise onto the pipe threads of the nipple. Using extra Teflon tape on the threads creates resistance if the spout tip points past six o'clock when tight.

3 Twist the new spout onto the nipple until it is flush against the wall and the spout is oriented properly. If the spout falls short of six o'clock, you may protect the finish of the spout with tape and twist it a little beyond hand tight with your channel-type pliers—but don't over do it; the fitting can crack.

Replacing a Widespread Bathroom Faucet

18

Three-piece (widespread) faucets are as classy as a good three-piece suit, and the styles are virtually unlimited.

WIDESPREAD FAUCETS COME IN THREE PIECES INSTEAD OF ONE: a hot tap, a cold tap, and the spout. Each piece is mounted separately in its own hole in the sink. The hot and cold taps (valves) are connected to hot and cold water supplies respectively. The spout is connected to the valves with reinforced flexible hoses. The great advantage to this configuration is that you gain flexibility when locating your spout and handles. If your faucet set has a long enough hose, you can even create arrangements such as locating the handles near one end of the tub and the spout near the other so you can turn the water on and off or adjust the temperature without getting up. Even models made for bathroom lavatories, like the one you see here, offer many creative configuration options.

TIP: Save your paperwork. Should you ever need to service your faucet, the product literature will be useful for troubleshooting and identifying and replacing parts.

WIDESPREAD FAUCETS 101

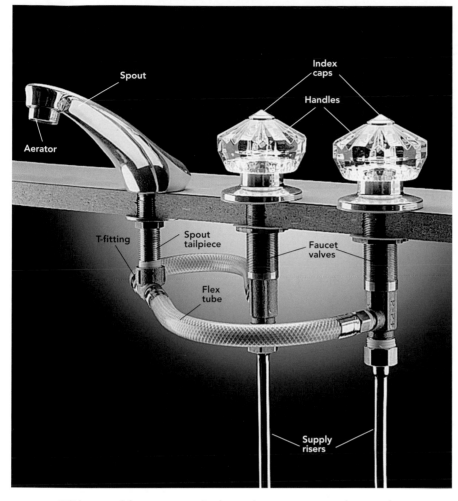

Spout

Index caps

Handles

Aerator

T-fitting

Spout tailpiece

Faucet valves

Flex tube

Supply risers

Widespread faucets come in three pieces, a *spout* and two *valves*. *Supply risers* carry hot and cold water to the valves, which are turned to regulate the amount of water going to the spout, where the water is mixed. Water travels from the valves to the spout through *flex tubes*, which attach to the *spout tailpiece* via a *T-fitting*. Three-piece faucets designed to work with a pop-up stopper have a *clevis* and a *lift rod* (see pages 126 to 129). The *handles* attach with *handle screws* that are covered with *index caps*. An *aerator* is screwed on the faucet spout after debris is flushed from the faucet.

TERMS YOU NEED TO KNOW

PLUMBER'S PUTTY—a soft clay-like material used to seal faucet parts to sink parts.

TEFLON TAPE—a thin, white tape used to lubricate and seal threaded fittings.

PIPE JOINT COMPOUND—a paste that may be used instead of Teflon tape.

LAVATORY—another name for a bathroom sink.

TOOLS & SUPPLIES YOU'LL NEED

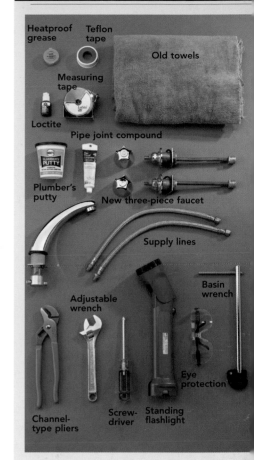

Heatproof grease

Teflon tape

Old towels

Measuring tape

Loctite

Pipe joint compound

Plumber's putty

New three-piece faucet

Supply lines

Adjustable wrench

Basin wrench

Channel-type pliers

Screw-driver

Standing flashlight

Eye protection

SKILLS YOU'LL NEED

• Using a basin wrench
• Working in confined spaces
• Making compression unions

DIFFICULTY LEVEL

SKILLS LEVEL

EASY   MODERATE

Time: 1 to 3 hours

HOW TO REMOVE A WIDESPREAD FAUCET

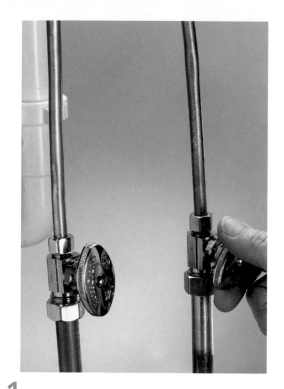

1 Clear out the cabinet under the sink and lay down towels. Turn off the hot and cold stop valves, and open the hot and cold taps. If you have difficulty turning the water off, turn to page 16.

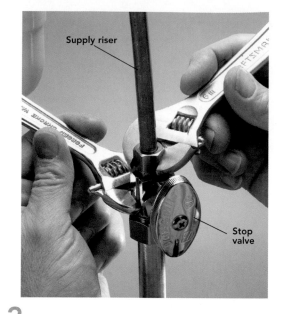

Supply riser

Stop valve

2 Unthread the compression nuts that connect the hot and cold supply risers to the stop valves. If a compression nut is frozen, stabilize the valve body with another wrench before applying more force.

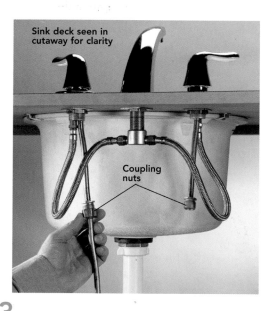

Sink deck seen in cutaway for clarity

Coupling nuts

3 Remove the coupling nuts holding the risers to the supply tubes from the faucet, stabilizing the tubes with a second wrench. Don't reuse old metal supply risers; the soft metal ends have been press-formed to the supply tubes of the old faucet.

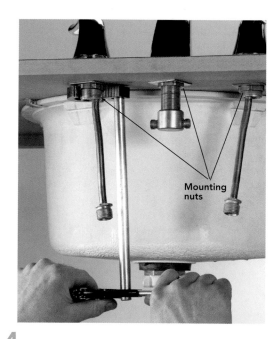

Mounting nuts

4 Using a basin wrench, disconnect all three mounting nuts holding the two faucet handles and the spout. You may need to have somebody hold the spout or valve steady from above. Remove the old faucet parts and clean the installation area in preparation for the new faucet.

HOW TO INSTALL A WIDESPREAD FAUCET

1 Insert the shank of the faucet spout through one of the holes in the sink deck (usually the center hole but you can offset it in one of the end holes if you prefer). If the faucet is not equipped with seals or O-rings for the spout and handles, pack plumber's putty on the undersides before inserting the valves into the deck. NOTE: If you are installing the widespread faucet in a new sink deck, drill three holes of the size suggested by the faucet manufacturer (see page 102 for tips on locating the holes).

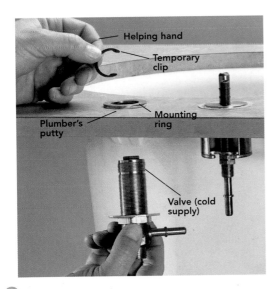

3 Mount the valves to the deck using whichever method the manufacturer specifies (it varies quite a bit). In the model seen here, a mounting ring is positioned over the deck hole (with plumber's putty seal) and the valve is inserted from below. A clip snaps onto the valve from above to hold it in place temporarily (you'll want a helper for this).

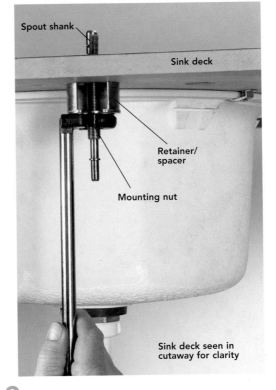

Sink deck seen in cutaway for clarity

2 In addition to mounting nuts, many spout valves for widespread faucets have an open retainer fitting that goes between the underside of the deck and the mounting nut. Others have only a mounting nut. In either case, tighten the mounting nut with pliers or a basin wrench to secure the spout valve. You may need a helper to keep the spout centered and facing forward.

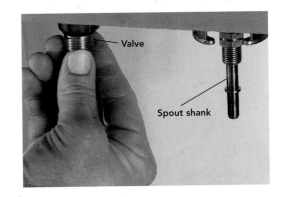

4 From below, thread the mounting nuts that secure the valves to the sink deck. Make sure the cold water valve (usually has a blue cartridge inside) is in the right-side hole (from the front) and the hot water valve (red cartridge) is in the left hole. Install both valves.

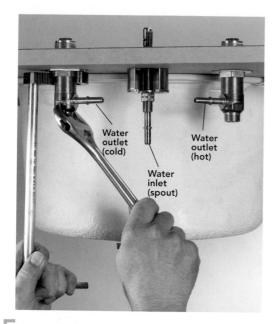

Water outlet (cold)

Water outlet (hot)

Water inlet (spout)

5 Once you've started the nut on the threaded valve shank, secure the valve with a basin wrench squeezing the lugs where the valve fits against the deck. Use an adjustable wrench to finish tightening the lock nut onto the valve. The valves should be oriented so the water outlets are aimed at the inlet on the spout shank.

T-fitting

6 Attach the flexible supply tubes (supplied with the faucet) to the water outlets on the valves. Some twist onto the outlets, but others (like the ones above) click into place. The supply hoses meet in a T-fitting that is attached to the water inlet on the spout.

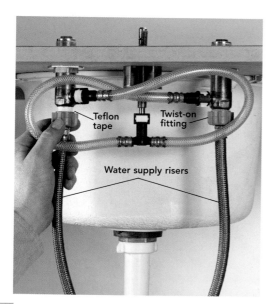

Teflon tape

Twist-on fitting

Water supply risers

7 Attach flexible braided metal supply risers to the water stop valves and then attach the tubes to the inlet port on each valve (usually with Teflon tape and a twist-on fitting at the valve end of the supply riser).

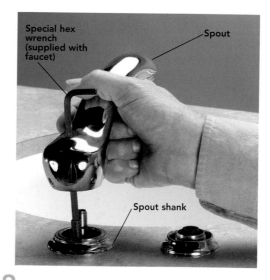

Special hex wrench (supplied with faucet)

Spout

Spout shank

8 Attach the spout. The model shown here comes with a special hex wrench that is threaded through the hole in the spout where the lift rod for the pop-up drain will be located. Once the spout is seated cleanly on the spout shank you tighten the hex wrench to secure the spout. Different faucets will use other methods to secure the spout to the shank.

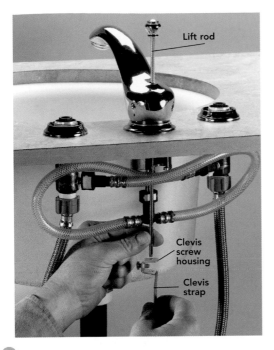

Lift rod

Clevis
screw
housing

Clevis
strap

9 If your sink did not have a pop-up stopper, you'll need to replace the sink drain tailpiece with a pop-up stopper body (often supplied with the faucet). See pages 120 to 125. Insert the lift rod through the hole in the back of the spout and, from below, thread the pivot rod through the housing for the clevis screw.

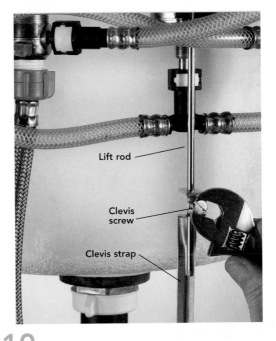

Lift rod

Clevis
screw

Clevis strap

10 Attach the clevis strap to the pivot rod that enters the pop-up drain body and adjust the position of the strap so it raises and lowers properly when the lift rod is pulled up. Tighten the clevis screw at this point. It's hard to fit a screwdriver in here, so you may need to use a wrench or pliers.

11 Attach the faucet handles to the valves using whichever method is required by the faucet manufacturer. Most faucets are designed with registration methods to ensure that the handles are symmetrical and oriented in an ergonomic way once you secure them to the valves.

Aerator

12 Turn on the water supply and test the faucet. Remove the faucet aerator so any debris in the lines can clear the spout.

Installing a
New Bathroom Faucet

19

Standard one-handle, deck-mounted bathroom faucets are interchangeable with two-handle models, fitting in the same two or three holes in the
bathroom sink.

ONE-PIECE BATHROOM FAUCETS ARE EASY TO REPLACE. They're attached to the
sink with a couple of mounting nuts and to the water supply with coupling nuts. With the
faucet gone, you'll be looking at two or three holes in the faucet deck. The outside holes take
tailpieces or mounting posts for the faucet, and the middle hole is for the pop-up stopper
lift rod. The outside holes are spaced four inches apart and will accept any standard deck-
mounted, one-piece bathroom faucet, except if you don't have a middle hole, you can't have
one with a pop-up stopper. We'd advise you to buy a heavy, quality faucet made of brass
(chrome or another metal on the outside). Cheap chromed-plastic faucets tend to wear out
at the handle attachments, and chrome-plated steel tends to rust. Faucets usually come with
a pop-up stopper mechanism. We show you how to replace these on pages 126 to 129.

ONE-PIECE FAUCETS 101

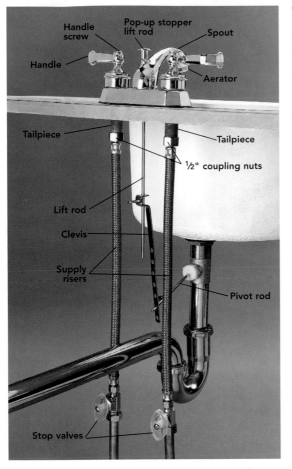

Handle screw
Pop-up stopper lift rod
Spout
Handle
Aerator
Tailpiece
Tailpiece
½" coupling nuts
Lift rod
Clevis
Supply risers
Pivot rod
Stop valves

The tailpieces of a standard deck-mounted, one-piece bathroom sink faucet are 4" apart on center. As long as the two outside holes in the back of your sink measure 4" from center to center, and you have a middle hole for a pop-up stopper, you can put in any standard one-piece bathroom faucet with *pop-up stopper.*

The faucet is secured to the sink with *mounting nuts* that screw onto the tailpieces from below. Also get two *flexible stainless steel supply risers* for sinks, long enough to replace the old tubes.

These typically attach to the stop valves with ⅜-inch *compression-sized coupling nuts* and to the faucet with standard *faucet coupling nuts.* But take your old tubes and the old compression nuts from the stop valves to the store to ensure a match. The *clevis, lift rod,* and *pivot rod* are parts of the pop-up stopper assembly. (Replaced on pages 126 to 129.) The handles attach with *handle screws* that are covered with *index caps.* An *aerator* is screwed on the faucet spout after debris is flushed from the faucet.

TERMS YOU NEED TO KNOW

PLUMBER'S PUTTY—a soft clay-like material used to seal faucet parts to sink parts.

TEFLON TAPE—a thin white tape used to lubricate and seal threaded fittings.

PIPE JOINT COMPOUND—a paste that may be used instead of Teflon tape.

DECK-MOUNTED FAUCET—another name for a one-piece faucet.

LAVATORY—another name for a bathroom sink.

TOOLS & SUPPLIES YOU'LL NEED

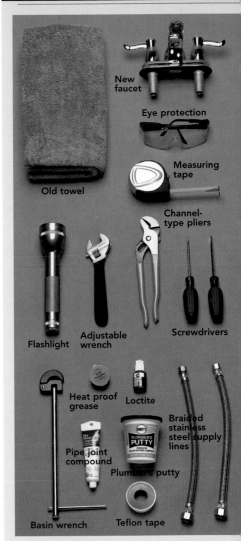

New faucet
Eye protection
Old towel
Measuring tape
Channel-type pliers
Flashlight
Adjustable wrench
Screwdrivers
Heat proof grease
Loctite
Braided stainless steel supply lines
Pipe joint compound
Plumber's putty
Basin wrench
Teflon tape

SKILLS YOU'LL NEED

• Making plumbing connections

• Ability to work in confined space

DIFFICULTY LEVEL

SKILLS LEVEL

EASY   MODERATE

TIME: 1 to 2 hours plus shopping

HOW TO REPLACE A ONE-PIECE FAUCET

1 Clear out the cabinet under the sink and lay down towels. Turn off the hot and cold stop valves and open the faucet. Unscrew the compression nuts that are holding the hot and cold supply tubes in the stop valves. Remove the coupling nuts holding the supply tubes to the tailpieces of the faucet and remove the tubes.

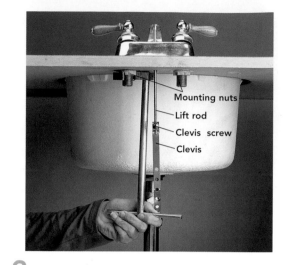

2 Put on protective eyewear! Debris will be falling in your face. Loosen the clevis screw (counterclockwise) holding the clevis strap to the lift rod. Remove the mounting nuts on the tailpieces of the faucet with a basin wrench or channel-type pliers. If the mounting nuts are rusted in place, apply penetrating oil, let stand ten minutes, and try again. TIP: Attach locking pliers to the basin wrench handle for greater leverage.

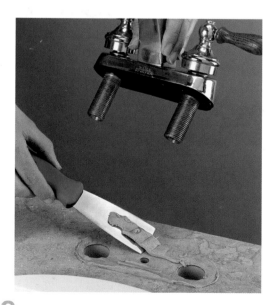

3 Pull the faucet body from the sink. Scrape off old putty or caulk with a putty knife and clean off the sink with a scouring pad and an acidic scouring cleaner like Barkeeper's Friend. Take your old supply tubes and the stop valve compression nuts to the home center so you'll know what size flexible supply risers to get.

4 Most faucets come with a plastic or foam gasket to seal the bottom of the faucet to the sink deck. These gaskets will not always form a watertight seal. If you want to ensure no splash water gets below the sink, discard the seal and press a ring of plumber's putty into the sealant groove built into the underside of the faucet body.

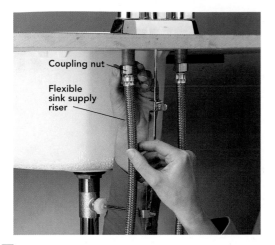

Coupling nut

Flexible
sink supply
riser

5 Insert the faucet tailpieces through the holes in the sink. From below, thread washers and mounting nuts over the tailpieces, then tighten the mounting nuts with a basin wrench until snug. Put a dab of pipe joint compound on the threads of the stop valves and thread the metal nuts of the flexible supply risers to these. Wrench tighten about a half turn past hand tight. Overtightening these nuts will strip the threads. Now tighten the coupling nuts to the faucet tailpieces with a basin wrench.

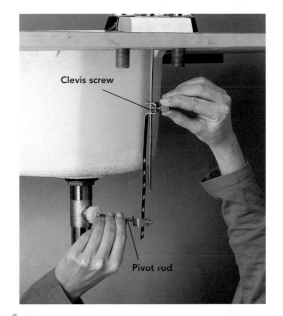

Clevis screw

Pivot rod

6 Slide the lift rod of the new faucet into its hole behind the spout. Thread it into the clevis past the clevis screw. Push the pivot rod all the way down so the stopper is open. With the lift rod also all the way down, tighten the clevis to the lift rod.

7 Grease the fluted valve stems with heatproof grease, then put the handles in place. Put a drop of Loctite on each handle screw before tightening it on. (This will keep your handles from coming loose). Cover each handle screw with the appropriate index cap—Hot or Cold.

8 Unscrew the aerator from the end of the spout. Turn the hot and cold water taps on full. Turn the water back on at the stop valves and flush out the faucet for a couple of minutes before turning off the water at the faucet. Check the riser connections for drips. Tighten a compression nut only until the drip stops.

Dealing with Kitchen Sprayers

20

When most of us think of kitchen sprayers, the image that comes to mind doesn't closely resemble the powerful stream of accurately directed water that's cleansing the fresh apples in the photo above. For a variety of reasons, sink sprayers seldom seem to function as designed. But improving the performance of your kitchen sprayer is a simple job with a high likelihood of success.

IF THE FLOW TO YOUR SPRAYER IS WEAK, first make sure the hose under the sink isn't kinked. If the hose is damaged, you will need to replace the hose and sprayer. If the screen at the base of the sprayer is clogged with debris, remove it and flush it clean. If you dislodged other parts from the base of the sprayer, clean these and put them back in the order in which they were removed. If the sprayer leaks from the base, replace the neoprene washer. If the sprayer doesn't turn off fully, replace the sprayer. If water isn't fully diverted from spout to sprayer, you may need to replace the diverter.

KITCHEN SPRAYERS 101

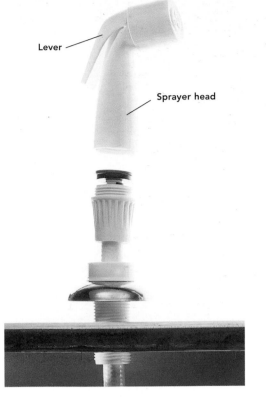

Lever

Sprayer head

When you squeeze the *lever* on your properly functioning kitchen sprayer, water flows out through the *sprayer head*, which causes a diverter valve in the faucet to close off water to the spout.

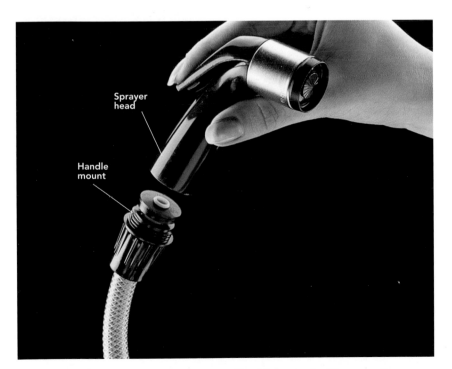

Sprayer head

Handle mount

Older spray hoses are easy to work with—you simply grasp the *sprayer head* and twist counterclockwise. The screen inside can then be removed and cleaned or replaced. Twist the sprayer head back on in a clockwise direction.

TOOLS & SUPPLIES YOU'LL NEED

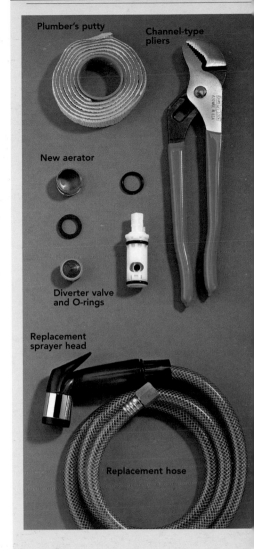

Plumber's putty

Channel-type pliers

New aerator

Diverter valve and O-rings

Replacement sprayer head

Replacement hose

SKILLS YOU'LL NEED

• Making pipe connections

• Working with putty

DIFFICULTY LEVEL

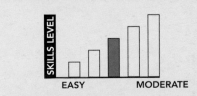

SKILLS LEVEL

EASY   MODERATE

Time: About an hour

HOW TO REPAIR A SPRAYER DIVERTER VALVE

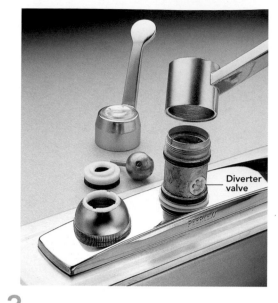

1 Shut off the water at the stop valves and remove the faucet handle to gain access to the faucet parts. Disassemble the faucet handle and body to expose the diverter valve. Ball-type faucets like the one shown here require that you also remove the spout to get at the diverter.

2 Locate the diverter valve, seen here at the base of the valve body. Because different types and brands of faucets have differently configured diverters, do a little investigating beforehand to try and locate information about your faucet. The above faucet is a ball type (see page 34).

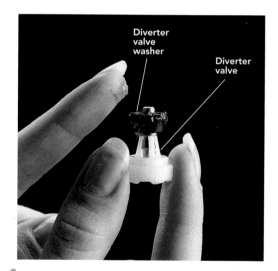

3 Pull the diverter valve from the faucet body with needlenose pliers. Use a toothbrush dipped in white vinegar to clean any lime buildup from the valve. If the valve is in poor condition, bring it to the hardware store and purchase a replacement.

4 Coat the washer or O-ring on the new or cleaned diverter valve with heatproof grease. Insert the diverter valve back into the faucet body. Reassemble the faucet. Turn on the water and test the sprayer. If it still isn't functioning to your satisfaction, remove the sprayer tip and run the sprayer without the filter and aerator in case any debris has made its way into the sprayer line during repairs.

HOW TO REPLACE A KITCHEN SPRAYER

1 To replace a sprayer hose, start by shutting off the water at the shutoff valves. Clear out the cabinet under your sink and put on eye protection. Unthread the coupling nut that attaches the old hose to a nipple or tube below the faucet spout. Use a basin wrench if you can't get your channel-type pliers on the nut.

2 Unscrew the mounting nut of the old sprayer from below and remove the old sprayer body. Clean the sink deck and then apply plumber's putty to the base of the new sprayer. Insert the new sprayer tailpiece into the opening in the sink deck.

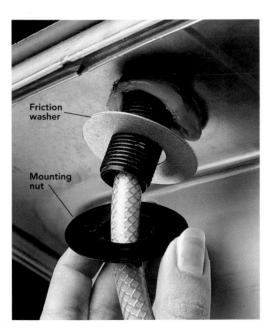

3 From below, slip the friction washer up over the sprayer tailpiece. Screw the mounting nut onto the tailpiece and tighten with a basin wrench or channel-type pliers. Do not over-tighten. Wipe away any excess plumber's putty.

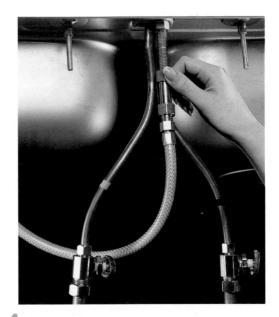

4 Screw the coupling for the sprayer hose onto the hose nipple underneath the faucet body. For a good seal, apply pipe joint compound to the nipple threads first. Tighten the coupling with a basin wrench, turn on the water supply at the shutoff valves, and test the new sprayer.

Repairing a Burst Pipe

21

Water supply pipes can burst for many reasons, but the most common cause is water freezing and expanding inside the pipe. First turn off the water, then apply a fix.

IF A WATER PIPE FREEZES AND BREAKS, your first priority may be getting it working again—whatever it takes. There are a number of temporary fix products out there, some involving clamps and sleeves, others, epoxy putties and fiberglass tape. These repairs usually can get you through a weekend okay. We also show you how to apply full slip repair couplings, a more permanent fix. Whatever repair approach you take, please, please, please, don't leave for the store without first determining a) the diameter of your pipe and b) the material of your pipe.

TIP: Pipes frozen? Don't let it happen again. Turn to page 94 to find out how.

WATER PIPE REPAIR PRODUCTS 101

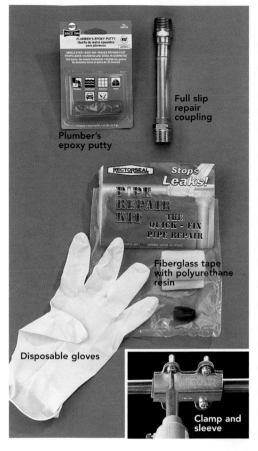

Plumber's epoxy putty

Full slip repair coupling

Fiberglass tape with polyurethane resin

Disposable gloves

Clamp and sleeve

Plumber's epoxy putty may stem a leak at a fitting, at least partially or temporarily. *Fiberglass tape with polyurethane resin* can produce a durable patch; it's sometimes used in conjunction with epoxy putty. A *clamp and sleeve* is quick and cheap. A *full slip repair coupling* is the closest to a permanent fix, but it requires straight and unblemished pipes of the right diameter and material. All of these products require that you carefully follow manufacturer's directions, or they simply will not work.

WARNING: A damaged pipe section with a patch should be replaced as soon as possible. Because of the natural movement of pipes, patches may leak again in time.

If a water supply pipe bursts, your first stop should be a shutoff. If there is a shutoff near the burst pipe, go ahead and turn off the water there or shut off the water to the whole house (right). Open faucets on every floor of the house to drain the supply system if your repair product requires dry pipe.

Metal file

Channel-type pliers

Adjustable wrench

Screwdriver

Tubing cutter

Tape measure

SKILLS YOU'LL NEED

- Using a tubing cutter
- Making compression joint

DIFFICULTY LEVEL

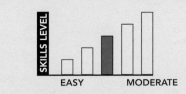

SKILLS LEVEL

EASY   MODERATE

Time: a few minutes plus shopping

TERMS YOU NEED TO KNOW

OUTSIDE DIAMETER—clamps and slip couplings require that you know the outside diameter of the pipe. Close an adjustable wrench on the pipe then measure the distance between the jaws.

PIPE MATERIAL—Certain repair products work on certain pipe types. Make sure you know yours before heading out to the home center.

HOW TO APPLY A SLEEVE AND CLAMP REPAIR

1 Make temporary repairs to a burst copper supply pipe with a sleeve clamp repair kit, available at most hardware stores. With the water supply shut off at the main, smooth out any rough edges around the damage with a metal file.

2 Center rubber sleeve of repair clamp over the rupture. If the sleeve enfolds the pipe, the seam should be opposite the rupture.

3 Place the two metal repair clamps around the sleeve.

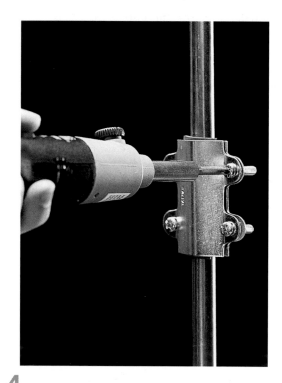

4 Tighten the screws with a Phillips screwdriver. Open water supply and watch for leaks. If it does leak, start from the beginning with the sleeve in a slightly different place. Have the section of ruptured pipe replaced as soon as possible.

HOW TO APPLY A REPAIR COUPLING TO A COPPER PIPE

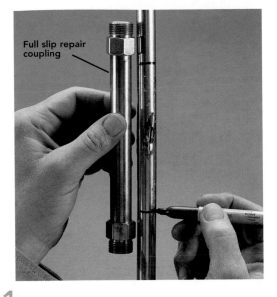

Full slip repair coupling

1 For a longer-lasting (not permanent) repair, use a compression-fit, full slip repair coupling (these come with parts to make a compression union—you can also buy a slip coupling that's just a piece of copper tubing with an inside diameter equal to the outside diameter of the tubing being repaired, but these require soldering). Turn off water at the meter. Mark the boundaries of the pipe to be replaced. This should include pipe beyond the damaged area. The cutout section must fall within the bare copper section of the repair coupling.

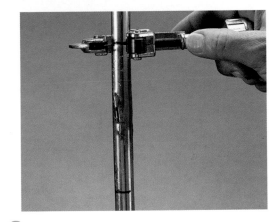

2 Lightly tighten the tubing cutter onto the pipe on a cutting line. Both wheels of the cutter should rest evenly on the pipe. Rotate the cutter around the pipe. The line it cuts should make a perfect ring, not a spiral. Tighten the cutter a little with each rotation until the pipe snaps. Repeat at your other mark.

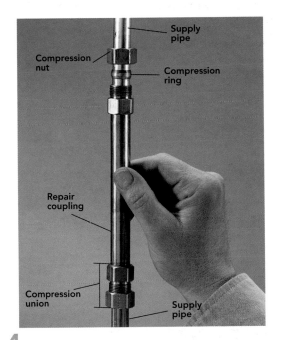

Supply pipe

Compression nut

Compression ring

Repair coupling

Compression union

Supply pipe

4 Slip the compression nuts and rings supplied with the repair coupling onto the cut ends of the pipe being repaired and then slip the repair coupling over one end. Slide the coupling further onto the pipe and then slide it back the other way so it fits over the other pipe section and the repair area is centered inside the coupling. Tighten each compression nut with pliers while stabilizing the coupling with an adjustable wrench.

3 Deburr the inside of the pipes with the triangular blade on the tubing cutter.

Replacing a Kitchen Faucet

22

Kitchen faucets don't last forever: in styling or in function. When it's time for you to say goodbye to yours, take comfort in knowing that if you choose one that's the same configuration, the project is quite simple.

MOST MODERN KITCHEN SINK FAUCETS ARE DECK MOUNTED, which means the bulk of the faucet sits on top of the back rim of the sink or counter. Typically, these faucets attach to the sink or counter and to their hot and cold water supplies through three holes. A fourth hole may hold a kitchen sprayer. Standard kitchen sinks (or pre-drilled counters) have three or four holes spaced 4" apart. It's best to look for a new faucet that uses the same number of holes as your current model, although any old holes that aren't used may be covered with a cap or a stand-alone accessory, like a liquid soap dispenser, that doesn't require additional plumbing work (there are several plumbed options, too, such as a water filter spout and a dishwasher air gap).

KITCHEN SINK FAUCETS 101

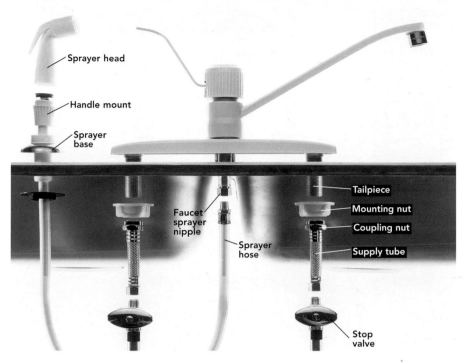

Sprayer head

Handle mount

Sprayer base

Faucet sprayer nipple

Sprayer hose

Tailpiece

Mounting nut

Coupling nut

Supply tube

Stop valve

In this section, we show you how to install one of the most popular faucet types for home use: a *single-lever kitchen sink faucet* with *hose sprayer,* configured for a four-hole sink with standard 4-inch spacing between the holes. If the faucet you want to install isn't quite the same type as this, keep reading anyway. The basic installation requirements are the same: the *faucet body* must be secured firmly to the sink or counter, and the *hot and cold supply tubes* must be connected to the *hot and cold water supplies.*

TERMS YOU NEED TO KNOW

COMPRESSION FITTING—a way of attaching copper tubes to stop valves.

FLEXIBLE SUPPLY LINES—flexible hoses that are used to attached to the hot and cold stop valves.

PLUMBER'S PUTTY—a soft clay-like material used to seal faucet parts to sink parts.

TEFLON TAPE—a thin, white tape used to lubricate and seal threaded fittings.

PIPE JOINT COMPOUND—a paste that may be used instead of Teflon tape.

DECK-MOUNTED FAUCET—a faucet that mounts on top of a sink or counter, usually in two to four holes spaced 4 inches on center.

TOOLS & SUPPLIES YOU'LL NEED

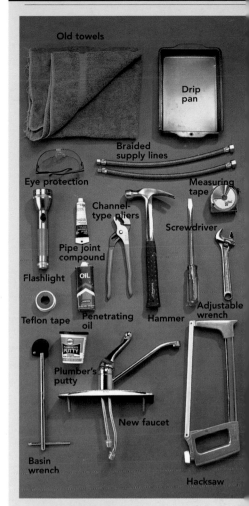

Old towels

Drip pan

Braided supply lines

Eye protection

Measuring tape

Channel-type pliers

Screwdriver

Pipe joint compound

Flashlight

Teflon tape

Penetrating oil

Hammer

Adjustable wrench

Plumber's putty

New faucet

Basin wrench

Hacksaw

SKILLS YOU'LL NEED

• Working with tools in tight spots
• Making compression joints

DIFFICULTY LEVEL

SKILLS LEVEL

EASY   MODERATE

Time: 2 to 3 hours for removal and installation plus shopping

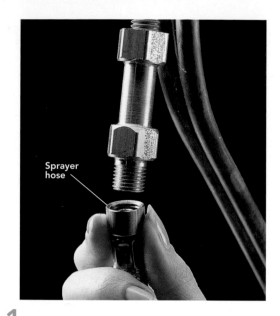

1 To remove the old faucet, start by clearing out the cabinet under the sink and laying down towels. Turn off the hot and cold stop valves and open the faucet to make sure the water is off. Detach the sprayer hose from the faucet sprayer nipple and unscrew the retaining nut that secures the sprayer base to the sink deck. Pull the sprayer hose out through the sink deck opening.

2 Spray the mounting nuts that hold the faucet or faucet handles (on the underside of the sink deck) with penetrating oil for easier removal. Let the oil soak in for a few minutes.

3 Unhook the supply tubes at the stop valves. Don't reuse old chrome supply tubes. If the stops are missing or unworkable, replace them. Then, remove the coupling nuts and the mounting nuts on the tailpieces of the faucet with a basin wrench or channel-type pliers.

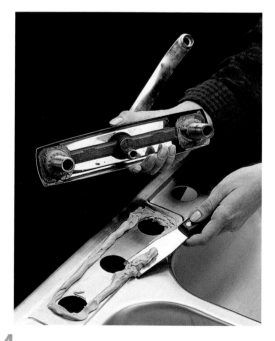

4 Pull the faucet body from the sink. Remove the sprayer base, if you wish to replace this. Scrape off old putty or caulk with a putty knife and clean off the sink with a scouring pad and an acidic scouring cleaner like Barkeeper's Friend.
TIP: Scour stainless steel with a back and forth motion to avoid leaving unsightly circular markings.

HOW TO INSTALL A KITCHEN FAUCET

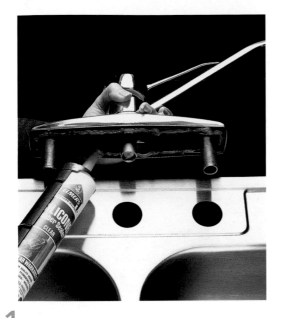

1 Apply a thick bead of silicone caulk to the underside of the faucet base then insert the tailpieces of the faucet through the appropriate holes in the sink deck. Press down lightly on the faucet to set it in the caulk.

SHOPPING TIP

Take a close look at the faucet material:

Under a pretty chrome finish a faucet may be brass, steel, or even plastic. A solid brass faucet with heavy brass handles will last longest. Regular (not stainless) steel will eventually rust, even if there is another metal on the top (brass- and chrome-plated steel nuts and screws are notorious for rusting into gobs of unmovable metal). Plastic or lightweight brass will wear out, especially where the handles attach to the valves.

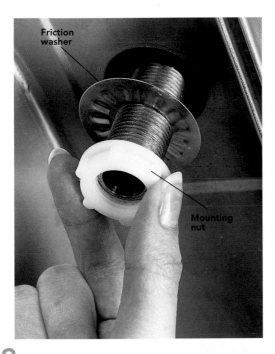

Friction washer

Mounting nut

2 Slip a friction washer onto each tailpiece and then hand-tighten a mounting nut. Tighten the mounting nut with channel-type pliers or a basin wrench. Wipe up any silicone squeeze-out on the sink deck with a wet rag before it sets up.

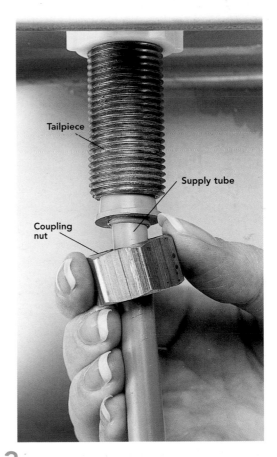

Tailpiece

Supply tube

Coupling nut

3 Connect supply tubes to the faucet tailpieces—make sure the tubes you buy are long enough to reach the stop valves and that the coupling nuts will fit the tubes and tailpieces.

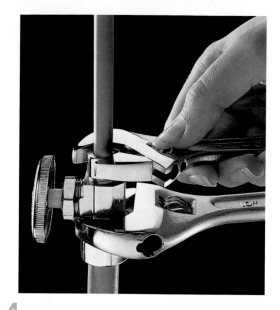

Sprayer
tailpiece

4 Attach the supply tubes to the shutoff valves, using compression fittings. Make sure you connect the hot supply to the hot stop valve. Hand-tighten the nuts, then use an adjustable wrench to tighten them an additional quarter turn. It's a good idea to hold the shutoff valve with another wrench to stabilize it while you tighten the nut. It's also a good idea to wrap some Teflon tape around the threads of the shutoff body.

5 Apply a ¼" bead of plumber's putty or silicone caulk to the underside of the sprayer base. With the base threaded onto the sprayer hose, insert the tailpiece of the sprayer through the opening in the sink deck.

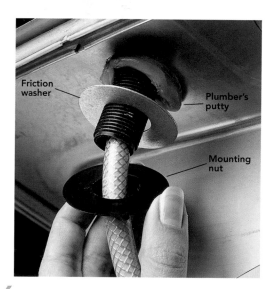

Friction
washer

Plumber's
putty

Mounting
nut

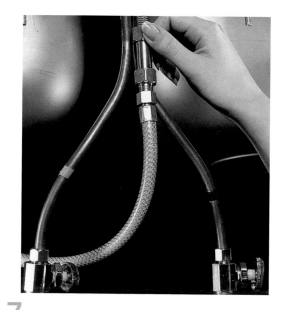

6 From beneath, slip the friction washer over the sprayer tailpiece and then screw the mounting nut onto the tailpiece. Tighten with channel-type pliers or a basin wrench. Wipe any excess putty or caulk on the sink deck from around the base.

7 Screw the sprayer hose onto the hose nipple on the bottom of the faucet. Hand-tighten and then give the nut one quarter turn with pliers or a basin wrench. Turn on the water supply at the shutoff, remove the aerator and flush debris from the faucet.

VARIATION: INSTALLING A KITCHEN FAUCET WITH PREATTACHED COPPER SUPPLY TUBES

1 Some faucets come with the copper supply tubes preattached to the faucet body. This minimizes the number of connections so you can hook the new faucet directly to the shutoff valves. To install a single-handle lever-type faucet with preattached supply tubes, start by caulking the faucet base and setting it on the deck, as in step 1, on page 123. The copper supply tubes and the sprayer nipple should go through the center hole and then mounting bolts on each side should go through the two outside holes.

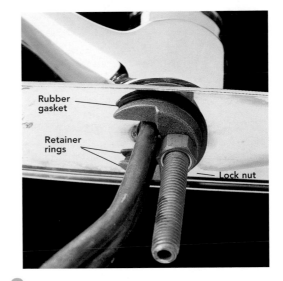

2 Secure the faucet to the sink deck by placing a rubber gasket between the retainer rings and the underside of the countertop. Orient the cutout in the retainer to fit around the supply tubes. Thread a lock nut onto the threaded sprayer nipple and hand-tighten up to the retainer.

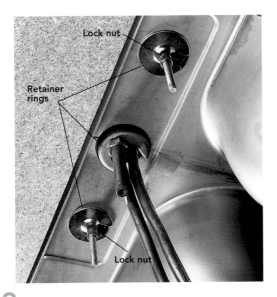

3 Attach retainer rings and washers to the two mounting bolts as well and hand-tighten the mounting nuts. Tighten all nuts with pliers or a basin wrench.

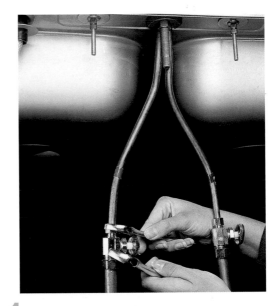

4 Bend the copper faucet tubes so they are in straight up-and-down positions as they meet the stop valves. You may need to trim them with a tubing cutter. Connect the tubes to the stop valves with compression nuts and rings (attach the hot supply tube to the hot supply pipe). Install the sprayer as shown on the previous page. Turn on the water at the shutoffs and test the faucet.

23

Replacing a Pop-up Stopper

A bum pop-up stopper may require complete regime change. Not just the stopper, but the tube and lever apparatus under it may need to be replaced.

POP-UP STOPPERS ARE THOSE CHROME-PLATED, LONG-LEGGED PLUGS IN BATH-ROOM SINKS that are opened and closed with a knob behind the spout. The stopper itself is just the glory guy for a behind-the-scenes assembly that makes sure the stopper sits and stands on cue. New faucets come with their own pop-up stopper assemblies, assuming they use one, but you may also purchase one by itself. This will include everything from the stopper to the pipe that drops into the trap (the trap is that drooping piece of drainpipe under your sink). If you choose to buy a pop-up stopper assembly, we recommend one that's heavy brass under the chrome finish. This will hold up better to time and abuse than a plastic or light-gauge metal model.

POP-UP STOPPERS 101

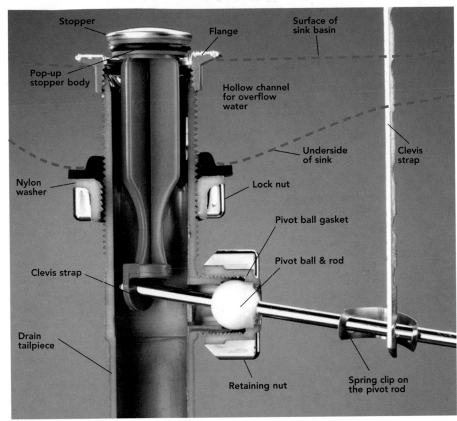

Stopper · Flange · Surface of sink basin
Pop-up stopper body · Hollow channel for overflow water
Nylon washer · Underside of sink · Clevis strap
Lock nut
Pivot ball gasket
Pivot ball & rod
Clevis strap
Drain tailpiece
Retaining nut · Spring clip on the pivot rod

Pop up stoppers keep objects from falling down the drain, and they make filling and draining the sink easy. When you pull up on the *lift rod*, the *clevis strap* is raised, which raises the *pivot rod*, which seesaws on the *pivot ball* and pulls the *pop-up stopper* down against the *flange*. This blocks water through the sink drain, but water may still overflow into the *overflow channel*, and get into the stopper body and down the drain through *overflow ports* in the pop-up body, which is a nice feature if you leave the water running in a plugged basin by mistake.

TERMS YOU NEED TO KNOW

PLUMBER'S PUTTY—a soft clay-like material used to seal metal parts to the sink.

TEFLON TAPE—a thin, white tape used to lubricate and seal threaded fittings.

PIPE JOINT COMPOUND—a paste that may be used instead of Teflon tape.

POP-UP WASTE—another term for a pop-up assembly.

TAILPIECE—takes the waste from the pop-up stopper body to the J-bend.

J-BEND—a J-shaped bend of drainpipe below the sink. It's the part of the trap that's always full of water to keep sewer gases from rising into the house.

TOOLS & SUPPLIES YOU'LL NEED

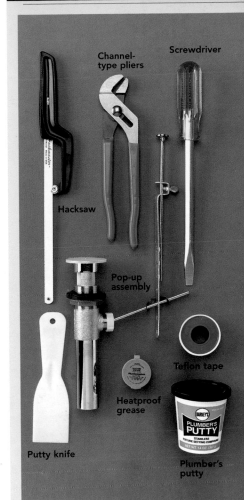

Channel-type pliers · Screwdriver
Hacksaw
Pop-up assembly
Teflon tape
Putty knife
Heatproof grease
Plumber's putty

SKILLS YOU'LL NEED

- Making slip joints
- Handling small parts
- Cutting metal with a hacksaw

DIFFICULTY LEVEL

SKILLS LEVEL

EASY · MODERATE

Time: 1 to 2 hours plus shopping

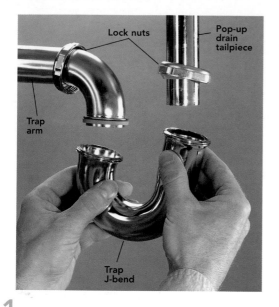

1 Put a basin under the trap to catch water. Loosen the nuts at the outlet and inlet to the trap J-bend by hand or with channel-type pliers and remove the bend. The trap will slide off the pop-up body tailpiece when the nuts are loose. Keep track of washers and nuts and their up/down orientation by leaving them on the tubes.

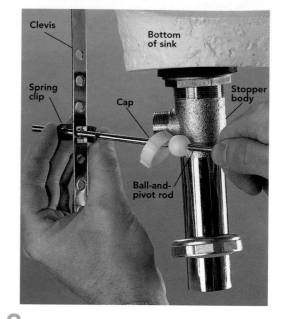

2 Unscrew the cap holding the ball-and-pivot rod in the pop-up body and withdraw the ball. Compress the spring clip on the clevis and withdraw the pivot rod from the clevis.

3 Remove the pop-up stopper. Then, from below, remove the lock nut on the stopper body. If needed, keep the flange from turning by inserting a large screwdriver in the drain from the top. Thrust the stopper body up through the hole to free the flange from the basin, and then remove the flange and the stopper body.

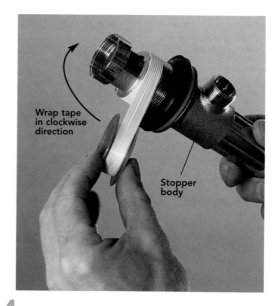

4 Clean the drain opening above and below, and then thread the locknut all the way down the new pop-up body followed by the flat washer and the rubber gasket (beveled side up). Wrap three layers of Teflon tape clockwise onto the top of the threaded body. Make a ½"-dia. snake from plumber's putty, form it into a ring and stick the ring underneath the drain flange.

Plumber's putty

5 From below, face the pivot rod opening directly back toward the middle of the faucet and pull the body straight down to seat the flange. Thread the locknut/washer assembly up under the sink, then fully tighten the locknut with channel-type pliers. Do not twist the flange in the process, as this can break the putty seal. Clean off the squeezeout of plumber's putty from around the flange.

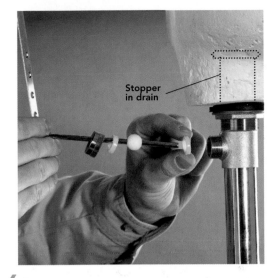

Stopper in drain

6 Drop the pop-up stopper into the drain hole so the hole at the bottom of its post is closest to the back of the sink. Put the beveled nylon washer into the opening in the back of the pop-up body with the bevel facing back.

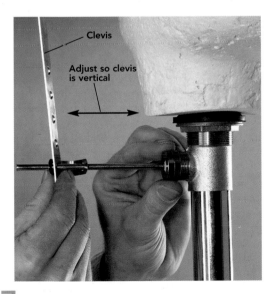

Clevis

Adjust so clevis is vertical

7 Put the cap behind the ball on the pivot rod as shown. Sandwich a hole in the clevis with the spring clip and thread the long end of the pivot rod through the clip and clevis. Put the ball end of the pivot rod into the pop-up body opening and into the hole in the the stopper stem. Screw the cap on to the pop-up body over the ball.

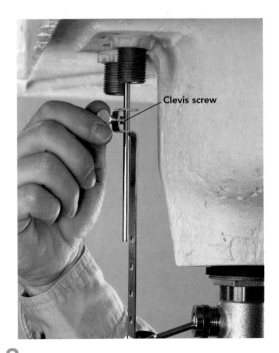

Clevis screw

8 Loosen the clevis screw holding the clevis to the lift rod. Push the pivot rod all the way down (which fully opens the pop-up stopper). With the lift rod also all the way down, tighten the clevis screw to the rod. If the clevis runs into the top of the trap, cut it short with your hacksaw or tin snips. Reassemble the J-bend trap.

24

Replacing a toilet is simple, and the latest generation of 1.6-gallon water-saving toilets has overcome the performance problems of earlier models.

YOU CAN REPLACE A POORLY FUNCTIONING TOILET WITH A HIGH-EFFICIENCY, HIGH-QUALITY NEW TOILET FOR UNDER TWO HUNDRED AND FIFTY DOLLARS, but don't, as Ben Franklin would say, be penny wise and pound foolish. All toilets made since 1996 have been required to use 1.6 gallons or less per flush, which has been a huge challenge for the industry. Today, the most evolved 1.6-gallon toilets have wide passages behind the bowl and wide (three-inch) flush valve openings—features that facilitate short, powerful flushes. This means fewer second flushes and fewer clogged toilets. These problems were common complaints of the first generation of 1.6-gallon toilets and continue to beleaguer inferior models today. See what toilets are available at your local home center in your price range, then go online and see what other consumers' experiences with those models have been. New toilets often go through a "de-bugging" stage when problems with leaks and malfunctioning parts are more common. Your criteria should include ease of installation, good flush performance, and reliability. With a little research, you should be able to purchase and install a high-functioning economical gravity-flush toilet that will serve you well for years to come.

TOILETS 101

Round front

Floor bolt (cap on)

Rough-in distance 10", 12" or 14" (12" most common)

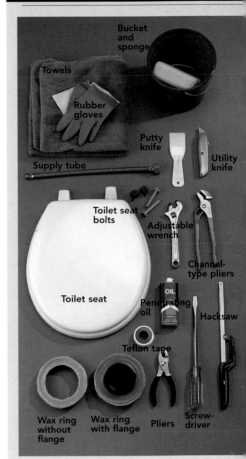
Buy a toilet that will fit the space. Measure the distance from the floor bolts back to the wall (if your old toilet has two pairs of bolts, go by the rear pair). This is your *rough-in distance* and will be either 10" or approximately 12". Make note of the *bowl shape*, round or oval (long). Oval bowls (also called elongated bowls) are a few inches longer for greater comfort, but may be too big for your space. The safest bet is to buy a replacement with the same bowl shape.

SKILLS YOU'LL NEED

- Making compression joints
- Lifting 50 pounds
- Hand tool usage

TERMS YOU NEED TO KNOW

CLOSET FLANGE—the metal or plastic slotted ring on the floor around the drain opening to which the toilet is bolted.

CLOSET ELBOW—the drain elbow the closet flange attaches to.

WAX RING—a compressible ring that forms a seal between the toilet and the closet flange; it fits either a 3-inch or 4-inch closet elbow.

CLOSET BOLTS—the pair of bolts that attach the toilet to the flange.

DIFFICULTY LEVEL

SKILLS LEVEL

EASY   MODERATE

Time: Allow about 1 hour for this project

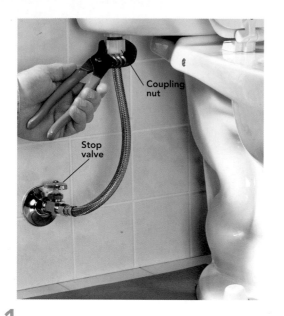

Coupling
nut

Stop
valve

1 Remove the old toilet. First, turn off the water at the stop valve (see page 18 if you have trouble). Flush the toilet holding the handle down for a long flush, and sponge out the tank. Unthread the coupling nut for the water supply below the tank using channel-type pliers if needed. TIP: If you have a wet vac, use this here and in step three to clear any remaining water out of the tank and bowl.

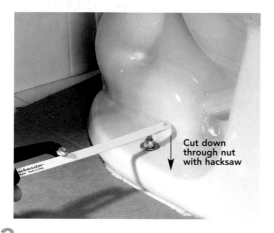

Cut down
through nut
with hacksaw

3 Remove the nuts that hold the bowl to the floor. First, pry off the bolt covers with a screwdriver. Use a socket wrench, locking pliers, or your channel-type pliers to loosen the nuts on the tank bolts. Apply penetrating oil and let it sit if the nuts are stuck, then take them off. As a last resort, cut the bolts off with a hacksaw by first cutting down through one side of the nut. Tilt the toilet bowl over and remove it.

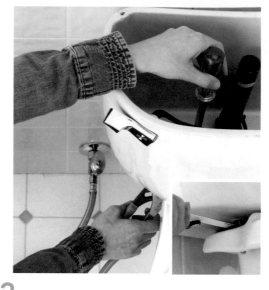

2 Grip each tank bolt nut with a box wrench or pliers and loosen it as you stabilize each tank bolt from inside the tank with a large slotted screwdriver. If the nuts are stuck, apply penetrating oil to the nut and let it sit before trying to remove them again. You may also cut the tank bolts between the tank and the bowl with an open-ended hacksaw (inset). Remove and discard the tank.

TECHNIQUE TIP

Removing an old wax ring is one of the more disgusting jobs you'll encounter in the plumbing universe (the one you see here is actually in relatively good condition). Work a stiff putty knife  underneath the plastic flange of the ring (if you can) and start scraping. In many cases the wax ring will come off in chunks. Discard each chunk right away—they stick to everything. If you're left with a lot of residue, scrub with mineral spirits. Once clean, stuff a rag in a bag in the drain opening to block sewer gas.

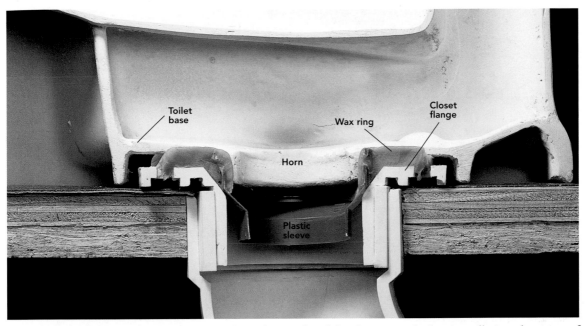

A cross-section of the connection between the toilet stool and the drain reveals that it really is only a ring of wax that makes the difference between a pleasant water closet and something that smells like an open sewer.

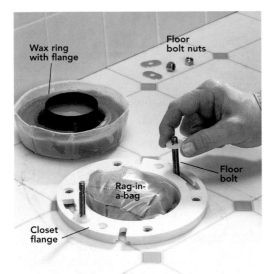

4 Remove the rag-in-a-bag from the drain opening and put new all-brass toilet bolts into the slots on the closet flange at 3 and 9 o-clock and rotate each ¼ turn so the elongated heads cannot be withdrawn. Put the plastic keepers or extra washers and nuts on the bolts to secure them to the flange. Unwrap the wax ring and position it over the flange so it looks like the one in the cross section photo at the top of this page.

5 Lower the new toilet down over the wax ring so the bolts go through the holes on the bottom of the stool (this can be tricky—be patient and get help). Press down on the toilet to seat it in the wax ring and check for level. If the bowl is not quite level, you can shim the low side with a few pennies. Thread washers and nuts onto the floor bolts and tighten them a little at a time, alternating. Do not overtighten. Cut the bolts off above the nuts with a hacksaw and add the caps. Lay a bead of tub and tile caulk around the base of the toilet, but leave the back open to let water escape so you'll know if there's ever a leak.

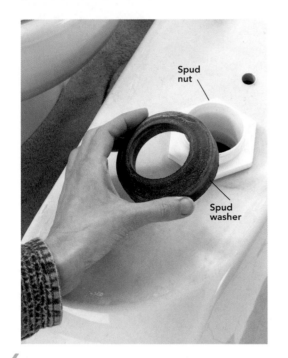

6 Attach the toilet tank. Some tanks come with a flush valve and a fill valve preinstalled, but if yours does not, insert the flush valve through the tank opening and tighten a spud nut over the threaded end of the valve. Place a foam spud washer on top of the spud nut.

7 If necessary, adjust the fill valve as noted in the directions (also see pages 54 to 57).

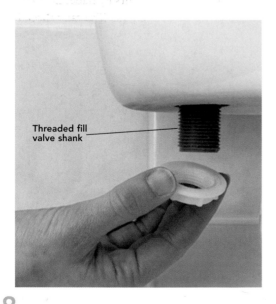

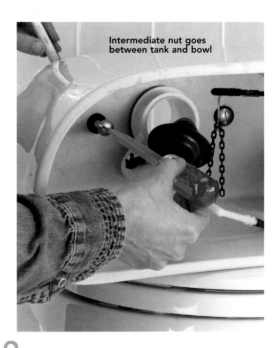

8 Position the valve in the tank. Push down on the valve shank (not the top) while hand-tightening the locknut onto the threaded valve shank (thread the nut on the exterior side of tank). Hand-tighten only.

9 With the tank lying on its back, thread a rubber washer onto each tank bolt and insert it into the bolt holes from inside the tank. Then, thread a brass washer and hex nut onto the tank bolts from below and tighten them to a quarter turn past hand tight. Do not overtighten.

10 Position the tank on the bowl, spud washer on opening, bolts through bolt holes. Put a rubber washer followed by a brass washer and a wing nut on each bolt and tighten these up evenly.

11 You may stabilize the bolts with a large slotted screwdriver from inside the tank, but tighten the nuts, not the bolts. You may press down a little on a side, the front, or the rear of the tank to level it as you tighten the nuts by hand. Do not overtighten and crack the tank. The tank should be level and stable when you're done.

12 Hook up the water supply by connecting the supply tube to the threaded fill valve with the coupling nut provided. Turn on the water and test for leaks.

13 Attach the toilet seat by threading the plastic or brass bolts provided with the seat through the openings on the back of the rim and attaching nuts.

Graduate School: Installing a Frost-free Faucet

25

That outside faucet freeze again? Replace it with one that you never have to turn off in the winter.

IF YOU LIVE IN A PART OF THE WORLD WHERE SUB-FREEZING TEMPERATURES OCCUR for extended periods of time, consider replacing your old sillcock (outdoor faucet) with a frost-proof model. In this project we show you how to attach the new sillcock using compression fittings, so no torch or molten solder is required. Compression fittings are ok to use in accessible locations, like between open floor joists in a basement. Your building code may prohibit their use in enclosed walls and floors. To see if your sillcock can be replaced according to the steps outlined here, see the facing page.

FROST-PROOF SILLCOCK 101

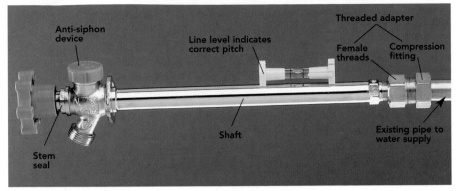

Anti-siphon device

Line level indicates correct pitch

Threaded adapter

Female threads

Compression fitting

Shaft

Existing pipe to water supply

Stem seal

The *frost-proof sillcock* shown here can stay active all winter because the stem washer turns off the water in the warm interior of the house. The *shaft* needs to be pitched slightly down toward the outside to allow water to drain from the shaft. This supply pipe is connected to the *threaded adapter* with a *compression fitting*, which is secured to the pipe with two wrenches.

Do not use the steps that follow if any of the following apply:

- Your pipes are made from steel instead of copper.
- The length of the pipe from the sillcock to where you can comfortably work on it is greater than 12 inches.
- The pipe has a valve or change of direction fitting within ten inches of the existing sillcock.
- The existing supply pipe is ⅝-inch outside diameter as measured with an adjustable wrench, and you are unable to make the hole in the wall bigger to accommodate the thicker shaft of the frost-proof sillcock. (For example, the hole is in a concrete foundation.)

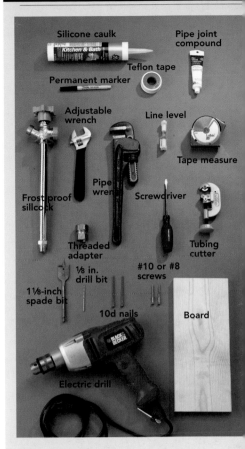
TERMS YOU NEED TO KNOW

SILLCOCK—an outdoor faucet with a threaded spout for a hose and a wide flange at the base allowing it to be attached to an exterior wall with screws.

FROST-FREE SILLCOCK—a sillcock with a long shaft that turns off the water inside the house.

COMPRESSION FITTING—a kind of mechanical pipe connection that allows copper pipes to be fitted without solder or a torch.

OUTSIDE DIAMETER (O.D.)—The outside diameter of the pipe is measured for a compression fitting.

NOMINAL DIAMETER—Valves, sillcocks, pipes, and fittings other than compression fittings go by the nominal diameter. For our purposes here, it's ⅛-inch less than the O.D.

SKILLS YOU'LL NEED

- Using a level
- Using a drill
- Using a tube cutter
- Making accurate measurements

DIFFICULTY LEVEL

SKILLS LEVEL

EASY   MODERATE

Time: 2 hours plus shopping

HOW TO REPLACE AN OUTSIDE FAUCET WITH A FROST-PROOF SILLCOCK

1 Turn off the water to your outside faucet at a shutoff found inside the house or basement behind the faucet (see page 18 if you have trouble turning off the water). Open the faucet and a bleeder valve on the shutoff to drain any remaining water from the pipe.

2 When you are sure the water flow has been stopped, use a tubing cutter to sever the supply pipe between the shutoff valve and the faucet. Make this first cut close to the wall. Tighten the tube cutter onto the pipe. Both wheels of the cutter should rest evenly on the pipe. Turn the cutter around the pipe. The line it cuts should make a perfect ring, not a spiral. If it doesn't track right, take it off and try in a slightly different spot. When the cutter is riding in a ring, tighten the cutter a little with each rotation until the pipe snaps.

Spot where supply tubing was cut

3/4" I.D. / 7/8" O.D.

3 Remove the screws holding the flange of the old sillcock to the house and pull it and the pipe stub out of the hole. Measure the outside diameter of the pipe stub. It should be either ⅝", which means you have ½" nominal pipe, or ⅞", which means you have ¾" nominal pipe. Measure the diameter of the hole in the joist. (If it's less than an inch, you'll probably need to make it bigger.) Measure the length of the pipe stub from the cut end to where it enters the sillcock. This is the minimum length the new sillcock must be to reach the old pipe. Record all this information.

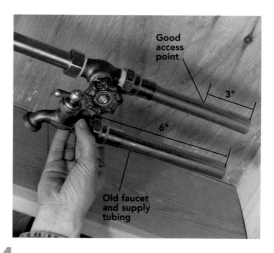

Good access point

3"

6"

Old faucet and supply tubing

4 Find a spot on the supply pipe where you have good access to work with a fitting and wrenches. The point of this is to help you select a new sillcock that is the best size for your project. In most cases, you'll have only two or three 6" to 12" shaft sizes to pick from. In the example above, we can see that the cut section of pipe is 6" long and the distance from the cut end to a spot with good access on the intact pipe is 3", so a new sillcock that's 9" long will fit perfectly.

Drill guide

5 If you need to replace old pipe with a larger diameter size, simplify the job of enlarging the sillcock entry hole into your home with a simple drill guide. First, drill a perpendicular 1⅛" diameter hole in a short board. From outside, hold the board over the old hole so the tops are aligned (you can nail or screw it to the siding if you wish). Run the drill through your hole guide to make the new, wider and lower hole in the wall.

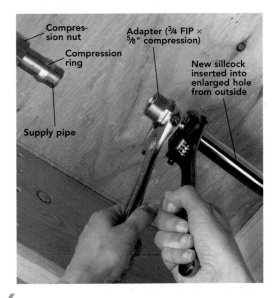

Compres-sion nut
Compression ring
Adapter (¾ FIP × ⅝" compression)
New sillcock inserted into enlarged hole from outside
Supply pipe

6 Insert the sillcock into the hole from the outside. Cut the supply pipe where it will meet the end of the sillcock. From the inside, wrap Teflon tape clockwise onto the threads of the sillcock. Stabilize the sillcock with one wrench and fully tighten the Adapter onto the threaded sillcock with the other wrench.

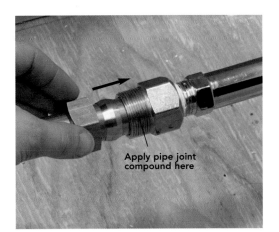

Apply pipe joint compound here

7 Insert the end of the supply pipe into the Adapter and pull them together. Spin the sillcock shaft so the faucet outside is oriented correctly (there should be a reference line on the bottom or top of the shaft). Apply pipe joint compound to the male threads on the Adapter body. Hand thread the nut onto the Adapter body. Stabilize the Adapter body with one wrench then tighten the compression nut with the other about two full turns past hand tight.

8 Turn the water back on. With the sillcock off and then on, check for leaks. Tighten the compression nut a little more if this union drips with the sillcock off. From outside the house, push the sillcock down against the bottom of the entry hole in the wall. Drill small pilot holes into the siding through the slots on the sillcock flange. Now, pull out on the sillcock handle in order to squeeze a thick bead of silicone caulk between the sillcock flange and the house. Attach the sillcock flange to the house with No. 8 or No. 10 corrosion resistant screws.

RESOURCES

American Standard Cos.
American Standard and Porcher
brand lavatories, toilets, shower
systems, bathtubs, kitchen
sinks, faucets
800-442-1902
www.americanstandard-us.com

Crane Plumbing
Crane, Fiat, Sanymetal,
Showerite and Universal
Rundle toilets and plumbing
products
www.craneplumbing.com

Delta Faucet Co.
Kitchen and bathroom faucets
800-345-3358
www.deltafaucet.com

Electric Eel
Power augers for sale or rent
(937) 323-4644
www.electriceel.com

Eljer Inc.
Eljer, Titan and Endurocast toilets, tubs, lavatories, faucets
800-423-5537
(972)560-2000
www.eljer.com

Elkay Cos.
Sinks and faucets
(630) 572-3192 (U.S.)
800-661-1795 (Canada)
www.elkayusa.com

Fluidmaster
Fill valves, flush valves, toilet
repair parts
www.fluidmaster.com

Grohe
Kitchen and bathroom faucets
(630) 582-7711 (U.S.)
(905) 271-2929 (Canada)

In-Sink-Erator
Garbages disposers and hot
water dispensers
800-558-5700
www.insinkerator.com

**International Association of
Plumbing and Mechanical
Officials**
20001 E. Walnut Drive South
Walnut, CA 91789-2825
www.iapmo.org

**International Conference of
Building Officials**
5360 Workman Mill Rd.
Whittier, CA 90601-2298
800-284-4406

Kohler Plumbing
Kohler brand kitchen and bathroom fixtures
800-456-4537
www.kohler.com

LASCO Bathware
Tub and shower products
800-9452726
www.lascobathware.com

Moen
Sinks, faucets and related
accessories for kitchen and
bath
800-289-6636
www.moen.com

**National Kitchens &
Bathroom Association**
(NKBA)
800-843-6522
www.nkba.com

**Plumbing and Drainage
Institute**
45 Bristol Drive
South Easton, MA 02375
www.pdionline.org

**Plumbing Heating Cooling
Information Bureau**
222 Merchandise Mart Plaza
Chicago, IL 60654
www.phcib.org

Price Pfister
Kitchen and bathroom faucets
800-732-8238 (U.S.)
800-340-7608 (Canada)
www.pricepfister.com

Sterling Plumbing
Sterling brand tub and shower
surrounds, shower doors, toilets,
kitchen sinks and related
kitchen and bathoom fixtures
888-783-7546
www.sterlingplumbing.com

The Institute of Plumbing
64 Station Lane, Hornchurch
Essex, RM12 6NM, England
www.worldplumbing.org

Toto USA Inc.
Toilets, faucets, lavatories and
and other bathroom fixtures
888-295-8134
www.totousa.com

INDEX

Also from
CREATIVE PUBLISHING INTERNATIONAL

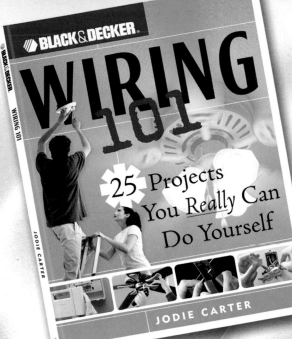

Wiring 101
25 Projects You Really Can Do Yourself

Save money and gain confidence by doing 25 of the most common wiring projects in your home. Even with little to no knowledge on the subject of wiring, you'll find the step-by-step instructions completely foolproof. Everything you need, from tools to finishing touches, is included to help make your wiring projects a success. You really can do this.

ISBN 1-58923-246-1

Flooring 101
25 Projects You Really Can Do Yourself

Your floors work hard, and deserve a little attention. With Flooring 101, you'll learn all about basic floor care—from keeping them clean and stopping squeaks, to repairing and replacing bad flooring. Included are 25 of the most common floor repair projects, including two simple installation projects for floors that are beyond repair. From concrete to carpet, hardwood to ceramic, parquet to vinyl, you'll find professional tips in easy-to-understand language to help you get the most out of your floors.

ISBN 1-58923-263-1

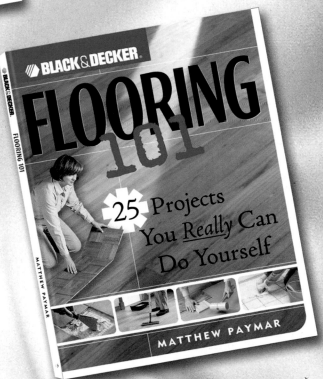

CREATIVE PUBLISHING INTERNATIONAL
18705 LAKE DRIVE EAST
CHANHASSEN, MN 55317
WWW.CREATIVEPUB.COM

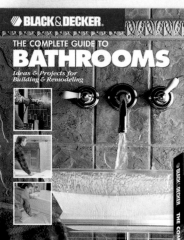

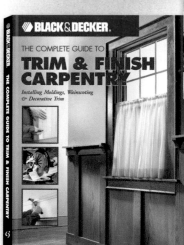